ANALECTA GORGIANA

Volume 13

General Editor

George Anton Kiraz

Analecta Gorgiana is a collection of long essays and short monographs which are consistently cited by modern scholars but previously difficult to find because of their original appearance in obscure publications. Now conveniently published, these essays are not only vital for our understanding of the history of research and ideas, but are also indispensable tools for the continuation and development of on-going research. Carefully selected by a team of scholars based on their relevance to modern scholarship, these essays can now be fully utilized by scholars and proudly owned by libraries.

Style and Language in the Writings of Saint Cyprian

Style and Language in the Writings of Saint Cyprian

E. W. Watson

Gorgias Press
2006

First Gorgias Press Edition, 2006

The special contents of this edition are copyright © 2006 by
Gorgias Press LLC

All rights reserved under International and Pan-American Copyright
Conventions. Published in the United States of America by
Gorgias Press LLC, New Jersey

This edition is a facsimile reprint of the
original edition titled "Style and Language of St. Cyprian" published in *Studia
Biblica et Ecclesiastica*, Oxford, 1896, vol. 4.

Analecta Gorgiana pagination appears in square brackets.

ISBN 1-59333-491-5

GORGIAS PRESS
46 Orris Ave., Piscataway, NJ 08854 USA
www.gorgiaspress.com

The paper used in this publication meets the minimum requirements of the
American National Standards.

Printed in the United States of America

THE STYLE AND LANGUAGE OF ST. CYPRIAN.

E. W. Watson

CHAPTER I.

THE STYLE OF ST. CYPRIAN.

§ 1. Introduction and Literature. § 2. Cyprian's works. § 3. Relation to the Old Latin Bible and other translations. § 4. Comparison with Tertullian. § 5. Comparison with Apuleius. § 6. Relation to Seneca and Cicero. § 7. Poetical and Gnomic elements. § 8. Cyprian's repetitions from himself. § 9 Tropes: metaphor, metonymy, periphrasis, hyperbaton, &c. § 10. Plays upon language. § 11. Symmetry. § 12. Grammatical devices for effect. § 13. Rhythm. § 14. Rhyme. § 15. Alliteration. § 16. Parataxis. § 17. Anaphora. § 18. Asyndeton. § 19. Amplification. § 20. Figura etymologica. § 21. Conclusion.

§ 1. Some six years ago the Bishop of Salisbury suggested to Mr. H. J. White and myself that we should turn our attention to the study of St. Cyprian. The work was begun, but Mr. White soon found that his work at the Salisbury Theological College and upon the Latin Vulgate would not permit him to share it. I have therefore had to continue it alone, but not without an interest and help from the Bishop and Mr. White, which have been of the greatest service, and indeed make Salisbury one of the few places in England where patristic studies can with any convenience be pursued.

Limits of space have compelled me to omit much that is interesting. All mention of syntactical matters[1], of the forms of words, of words which occur in writers of the same

[1] There is one instance of an auxiliary verb which is so remarkable that it must not be passed over: the earliest use of *uelle* as a future auxiliary in 484. 1 *addiderunt (martyres) . . . non in hoc fidere ut liberari in praesentia uellent sed illam libertatis et securitatis aeternae gloriam cogitarent.* The

class as Cyprian, has had to be abandoned, except where they illustrate the subject of the paper. Yet I hope that I have been able in some instances to improve and elucidate the text, and that the collection of words used by Cyprian in Christian senses may do something towards making the history of Christian terminology more definite, and the account of his style and rhetoric be of interest to those who are engaged upon the same subjects in other authors.

The exact object of this paper is to describe the chief characteristics of the style of St. Cyprian, to determine his literary affinities, and to collect the most remarkable words in his vocabulary, both general and theological. In all these respects his works offer much that is interesting and important for the history of the Latin literature and language, as well as for that of the growth of Christian thought and organization.

Little has as yet been done in these respects for the study of Cyprian. The great scholars of the seventeenth century who have edited him, though all, especially Rigault and Fell, with Dodwell in his wonderful *Dissertationes Cyprianicae*, have done good service, took little interest in the history of style and language. It is indeed remarkable that with their vast knowledge they should have passed over so much that is strange and striking. More may be learned from scattered notes in the works of such writers as Gronovius and Barth than from them. The progress that has been made of late has been considerable. The index to Professor von Hartel's edition in the Vienna Corpus of the Latin Fathers is in itself an admirable commentary, and the suggestions as to interpretation which it contains are indispensable to the student; but it was one of the earliest works to appear (1868–1871) in the Vienna edition, and like the rest of those first volumes it has a somewhat incomplete index. It can never be used to prove a negative, and cannot be regarded as an adequate authority for such inquiries as have been instituted by Professor Wölfflin, and now are

instance from Corippus given by Sittl, *Lokale Verschiedenheiten*, p. 128, is three hundred years later.

carried on by so many skilled colleagues of his in the *Archiv für lateinische Lexicographie* and elsewhere.

Two works upon the language of Cyprian have appeared of late years. One is very short, but admirable as far as it goes; the introduction prefixed to the Abbé Léonard's edition of some of the treatises [1], which, with his editions of Minucius Felix and Tertullian's *Apology*, ought to be better known in England. But this introduction, brief as it is, is mainly devoted to syntax, and on most points of style is altogether silent. The other work, of much greater size and far less value, is by the Abbé Le Provost [2]. It shows a very slight knowledge of modern scholarship and is quite without method; words and constructions, for instance, taken from Cyprian's Biblical citations, are arranged and discussed indiscriminately among Cyprian's own. Though the book contains a good deal that is useful, especially on pp. 61 ff., where the writer notices some of Cyprian's debts to Seneca and others, it is so discursive and in places so inaccurate as to be of little service, even had the author followed a better plan and possessed a wider knowledge [3].

But the chief debt of this paper is to the *Archiv für lateinische Lexicographie*, already mentioned, without the help and example of which, direct and indirect, it could not have been written. A special acknowledgement is due to Professors Wölfflin, Thielmann, and Landgraf for their work in that review and elsewhere [4]. Paucker, Rönsch, and many more

[1] *Sancti Thascii Cypriani Libri ad Don., de Mort., ad Demetr., de Bono Pat.*, édition classique ... par l'Abbé Ferd. Léonard; Namur, 1887.

[2] *Étude philologique et littéraire sur Saint-Cyprien*, par M. Le Provost, vicaire capitulaire de Saint Brieuc et Tréguier; Saint Brieuc and Paris, 1889, 304 pp., 8vo.

[3] One of his chief aims is to prove that Cyprian's writings and the Latin Bible, which he seems to regard as one of Cyprian's works, are almost Augustan in form.

[4] I may mention that some writers in the *Archiv*—not those mentioned nor others among its leading contributors—have used Hartel's index without looking to see whether the passages cited were Cyprian's own or from Cornelius or some other writer, and that Roman words have been in consequence attributed to Africa, and other false conclusions drawn.

192 The Style and Language of St. Cyprian.

who have dealt with the language generally or with particular writers, are mentioned in the following pages. To them, and to others who have suggested thoughts none the less valuable that there has been no occasion to cite their words, the heartiest thanks are paid [1].

§ 2. In this paper the works of Cyprian have been regarded as a whole. Written as they were within a period of ten years, and by a man whose style had been formed before his conversion to Christianity, there was no room for development in manner. All that his religion did for him was to change his subjects and to enlarge his vocabulary. It has often been said that his letters are more carelessly written than his treatises. There is some truth in this, though there is much bad writing in the latter [2]. On the other hand Cyprian's best and most elaborate writing, rhetorical and poetical, may be found in such panegyrical orations as *Epp.* 38, 39, 40, written to be pronounced before the assembled Church of Carthage on behalf of newly ordained clergy, as

---

[1] Schmalz's *Stilistik* in Iwan Müller's *Handbuch* has been of the greatest help. If it could be expanded to an adequate extent it might fulfil all requirements. The lines are laid down for a complete history of the growth of Latin style. Several years' continuous work have assured me more and more of the value of Georges' Lexicon. It would be ungrateful not to mention also the names of Sittl, Miodoński and Koffmane. Becker, Kretzschmann and Koziol, the writers on Apuleius, the author most akin to Cyprian in style, have been of great service. On Tertullian I have only seen the excellent paper by Kellner in the *Theol. Quartalschrift*, 1876, and Kolberg's and Bonwetsch's writings.

[2] E. g. 226. 10 *constituere audet aliud altare . . . nec scire quoniam* sq., 250. 19 *ante est ut sciamus . . . tunc facere* sq., 352. 19 *dixisti per nos fieri et quod nobis debeant imputari omnia ista*, 373. 19 *nisi iterum pietas diuina subueniens iustitiae et misericordiae operibus ostensis uiam . . . aperiret*, 386. 1 *ad corroborationem fidei et dilectionem Dei*, 405. 13 *unusquisque cum nascitur . . . initium sumit a lacrimis et quamuis adhuc omnium nescius et ignarus nihil aliud nouit . . . quam flere*, 408. 18 *ut fratri in te peccanti non tantum septuagies septies sed omnia omnino peccata dimittas*, 422. 9 *Saul quoque rex ut Dauid odisset . . . quid aliud quam zeli stimulus prouocauit?* 220. 25 f., 250. 12 f., 385. 10 f., &c. Tenses are constantly confused and put in wrong sequences; 197. 14, 239. 6, 260 3, 329. 16, 330. 20, 384. 13, 401. 1, 429. 14, &c. Indicative often in dependent clauses; 339. 18, 392. 20 f., 419. 10, &c.

Epp. 6, 10, 28 and 37, laudations of the Confessors, or *Ep.* 58 to the people of Thibaris, which Ebert[1] describes as showing the most brilliant and characteristic aspect of Cyprian's style. Such letters, if they ought to be so called, are hardly less ornate than the *Ad Donatum*. On the ground, then, of the substantial identity of Cyprian's style throughout his writings no distinction has been made between different parts of them in this paper, and all are cited simply by page and line of Hartel's edition.

All Cyprian's undoubted works are reviewed here. *Ep.* 33, of which some doubts have been expressed, has been included, though of course it can contribute little. But the *Quod Idola Dii non sint* has been excluded. There has been much discussion as to its genuineness, which there is no room to recapitulate here. It must suffice to say that its jerky style, its paucity of conjunctions, the want of any reference to it, and of any repetition of its language in other parts of Cyprian's writings. though he so constantly repeats what he regards as happy phrases, together with the use of terms which he never employs[2], have convinced me that it is not his. Yet even if the treatise be genuine, the loss to a knowledge of Cyprian through its exclusion is not great. It is a mere cento from known and perhaps unknown sources, much more clumsily compiled than Cyprian's adaptations from Tertullian[3]. In spite of the advocacy of Wölfflin and Matzinger, I have not felt justified in using the *De Spectaculis*

---

[1] *Litteratur des Mittelalters*, p. 63. He selects § 9 for special commendation. *Ep.* 11. § 8 is at least its equal. Goetz, *Gesch. d. Cypr. Litteratur*, Basel, 1891, gives a good collection of ancient opinions on Cyprian's excellence as an orator and writer.

[2] E. g. *altare* of a heathen altar 24. 14, *uulgus* 19. 2, 23. 11, 25. 10, 26. 18. The subject is mentioned in various notes in the following pages

[3] Jerome's witness (*Ep.* 70. 5) is the strongest claim that *Quod Id.* has to Cyprianic authorship. But quite apart from the question of the value of Jerome's attestation, which is not too great, it is clear that spurious treatises had been fathered on Cyprian a generation earlier. Lucifer's use of the *De Laudibus Martyrii* shows that he had no doubt of its being Cyprian's work, and it has a place in the Cheltenham List. *Qvod Id.* may well have no stronger claim, quite apart from internal evidence.

and *De Bono Pudicitiae* as Cyprianic [1]; but they again could not have contributed much material.

The text followed has of course been Hartel's. Little more can remain to be done for the Treatises, and the reader feels himself perfectly safe with that text [2]. But the Letters need much further investigation. There must be more meaning than has yet been discovered in the varying order of the *Epp.* in different groups of MSS., and even in MSS. closely allied, and more MSS. need to be collated [3]. But even so the changes to be made cannot be considerable.

§ 3. The most obvious characteristic of Cyprian's writings is their thoroughly rhetorical character, and their independence of Christian literary tradition. There were two considerable bodies of literature with which he might have shown affinity, the Old Latin Bible and its kindred translations from the Greek, and the writings of Tertullian. Of both his style shows independence, and of the former his constant attempt to improve upon the translators' Latin shows how little esteem he had for their work.

One cannot help being struck by the small respect which Cyprian shows for the language of his Latin Bible [4], which he quotes so constantly and so precisely. Apart from the

---

[1] Wölfflin on *De Spect.* in *Archiv für lat. Lex.* viii, p. 1; Matzinger, *Des hl. Cyprianus Tractat De bono Pudicitiae*, Nurnberg 1892. Each writer defends both treatises, and both can allege very strong grounds, though Matzinger's proofs seem the more convincing. But the arguments of Weyman (*Hist. Jahrbuch d. Gorres Gesellschaft*, 1892), Demmler (*Theol. Quartalschrift*, 1894) and Haussleiter (*Theol. Literaturblatt*, 1894) raise serious difficulties. Their claim for Novatian of these two tracts and of *Quod Idola* is less successful than their attack on Cyprian's authorship. It seems impossible that the same pen could have written both *Quod Idola* and the other two.

[2] With the well-known exception of the *Testimonia*.

[3] Cf. Professor Sanday in *Studia Biblica et Ecclesiastica*, III. p. 217 ff., on the Cheltenham List. On p. 299 is a table giving a partial clue to the arrangement of letters. In *Old Latin Biblical Texts* II, Appendix II, the same writer has given some account of the Oxford MSS, and shown reason for supposing them well worth further examination. I have lately collated those that seem most important.

[4] May I state my own strong conviction, for what it is worth, that there never was more than one original Old Latin version?

termini technici of Christian doctrine and discipline, and from his own diction when alluding to Scriptural, and especially Pauline, language, there is no sign of any dependence. In spite of its rich vocabulary, in some respects superior to that of the Vulgate, the Old Latin version was clumsily executed and quite modern. By his extreme care in indicating that its words are not his own (see p. 252), Cyprian seems to disclaim all responsibility for the translation which he had to use, and indeed its whole style is markedly incongruous with his own. There are a few Biblical phrases which he uses constantly and naturally, such as *accipere personas, ambulare in lumine, conuersatio, scandalum, tribulatio*. But their character shows that they were part of the common Christian vocabulary, as they had been, no doubt, before the Bible was translated into Latin [1]. But Cyprian not only, as a rhetorician, disliked the style of the Latin Bible: he was also discontented with its vocabulary. It used many Greek words; on a later page those which Cyprian retained are collected, and it will be seen with what vigour, and in some cases with what success, he strove to eject them. Indeed, the whole of the next chapter, dealing with his ecclesiastical vocabulary, is an evidence of his purism in this respect. He wrote a long letter (*Ep.* 63) upon the Eucharist, without ever using the word *eucharistia*; *daemon, mysterium*, and others are almost banished, and throughout his works he never uses words so common as *Paracletus, parabola, proselytus, neophytus, brauium*, though Tertullian freely used them all. The only Greek words, for which substitutes had been provided, which he constantly prefers are *baptisma*, because of heretical associations of *tinctio* (see p. 264), *presbyter*, because of the indefiniteness of *senior*, and *laicus* instead of *plebeius*. And there are few of the Greek terms of Church use for which he has not essayed to

---

[1] It would be interesting to know when the Latin Bible, for its own sake, became venerable in the eyes of Christians. Lactantius seems to have as little respect for it as Cyprian, and Arnobius even less. His allusions to definitely Christian matters are expressed in thoroughly unbiblical language. But in Jerome, Ambrose and Augustine a reverence for manner as well as for matter is evident.

find a Latin synonym. But it is not only Greek words which are avoided by Cyprian. He is still more averse to Hebrew. *Satan* and *Satanas*, common in Tertullian, are entirely absent. The only Hebrew word freely used is *gehenna* (374. 8, 483. 8, &c.). *Mamona*, 381. 18, *sabbatum*, 720. 2, and a few more could not be avoided [1].

But Latin words of modern or rude invention are disliked by Cyprian as much as Greek or Hebrew. The reader of the titles of the *Testimonia* finds himself in the presence of words quite different from those which Cyprian elsewhere employs; theological terms found only there or perhaps also in the carelessly written letters of the Baptismal controversy, which formed part of the original stock, but offended Cyprian's taste. Thus *saluator* only occurs *Test.* ii. 7 tit. and *saluare* only in the Baptismal letters, 790. 20, 809. 12, just as *catecumenus* is found in both *Test.* iii. 98 and 795. 16, and not elsewhere. *Saluare* was modern and probably undignified in sound; Cyprian's many substitutes for it will be found in Ch. II. The most noteworthy is the old ceremonial term of heathen worship, *sospitare*, 188. 25, 211. 9. Arnobius, 2. 74, another rhetorician, uses *sospitator* of Christ. Cyprian's use of this word, of *altare* for the *ara* of the O. L., of *uestigium* for *pes* in the Baptismal ceremony of washing and kissing the feet, for all of which see the next chapter, was no doubt part of a deliberate plan for making Christian language more stately, and so recommending the Faith.

Cyprian's extensive use of the Bible is certainly in part rhetorical. He renounced the direct citation of the classical

---

[1] Greek and Hebrew words are marked as alien by their not being adapted to Latin forms. The pl and acc. of *haeresis* and *exhomologesis* should probably always be in *-is* and *-in*; cf. 227. 14, 423. 11, 524. 6, 781. 10, 800. 1, 805. 21, 806. 9; *haereseos* 772. 17; *martyras* 502. 19, &c. *Propheten* seems the normal form, as in Tertullian Yet *agapem* 102. 5. Hebrew nouns, except those which are classical in form, as *Pharao* 328. 5, and *Daniel, Ezechiel*, &c., of the third declension (yet *Samuel* acc. 728. 20), are treated irregularly; e.g. *Abraham* is indeclinable 468. 19, 670. 6, 703, 19, but declined 704. 3, which, however, is Biblical. *Hierosolyma* (pl.) 660. 11, *Hierusalem* never.

writers, though he still employed them for ornamental allusions, and Scripture had to fill the place. It would be a very inadequate account of his motives to say that the *Testimonia* and *Ad Fortunatum* were composed for this end [1], but it would be easier to underestimate than to overestimate the rhetorical use made by Cyprian of his Bible, and especially of his own extracts in the *Testimonia*. The influence of this work over Christian literature for some generations after its compiler's death has probably not yet been realized. Yet when Cyprian himself is aiming at effect by means of florid diction, not by appeal to authority, he judiciously abstains from any suggestion of Biblical language.

There is some evidence that Cyprian knew Irenaeus (Harnack, *Altchristliche Literatur*, p. 267), and it may be more than an accident that the words *praefiguratio* 763. 14, and *plasma* 468. 12 should apparently occur for the first time in Irenaeus (5. 29, 2; and 1. 18, 5. 11, 2), and then in Cyprian, though not in Tertullian. But there is no evidence that he knew any other translations into Latin [2].

§ 4. Of Cyprian's dependence on Tertullian, his master according to Jerome's well-known anecdote, there can be no doubt. But it is entirely a dependence of matter, not of manner. No two styles can be more different. Tertullian is always concise, even to obscurity. His sentences, according to his own rules of art, are always well shaped; he can never be accused of carelessness. But he is the most reckless of writers in the adoption of words of vulgar life, and in their

---

[1] Yet cf. Haussleiter's *Cyprianstudien* in *Comment. Woelfflin*, p. 379 ff. Speaking of the *De Habitu Virginum* he says, 'Der fruhere Lehrer der Beredsamkeit benutzt die Sammlung der "Zeugnisse" unter dem rhetorischen Gesichtspunkt der Topik;' and later 'Der kasuelle Anlass, d e nothwendig gewordene Zurechtweisung der Virgines, bildet den Zettel des Gewebes. Den Einschlag liefern die *Testimonia* und der unerschopfliche Tertullian. Cyprian's Arbeit beschrankte sich so auf die rhetorische Ausfuhrung.'

[2] He may have known the Greek Irenaeus, not the Latin, which shows some signs of a later date. He certainly had a hand in the translation of *Ep* 75, though that can only have been in improving a Latin version already made.

198 *The Style and Language of St. Cyprian.*

invention for any momentary need. Cyprian, on the other hand, attains his effect by an amplitude of expression which degenerates often enough into mere verbosity, and is guilty from time to time of a sentence so prolonged and involved that its construction is lost or obscured. Indeed, he is a very careless writer, even at his best, as regards structure. Yet he is sparing in the use of new or colloquial words, and when he employs them it is almost always to obtain some rhetorical effect. For that purpose he is not afraid to endanger his sense, as will be seen from the passages given hereafter of language forced for alliteration, rhyme, &c.[1] Few of the words which strike the reader as characteristic of Tertullian are found, except in isolated instances, in Cyprian. Oehler's index under the headings, for example, of *adsignare, capere, censeri, conuenire, deputare, dispungere, elogium,* and many more, shows words and idioms of frequent occurrence that are never, or

---

[1] See pp. 222, 225, &c. In 728. 11 ff. is a question lost in a string of citations. *Ep.* 41 begins with two sentences, one of twenty and the other of fifteen lines. Instances of grammatical carelessness in the Treatises have already been given on p 192. The Letters have naturally even more errors. Some of his chief causes of confusion, beside those mentioned there, are the dependence of several clauses on one conjunction not repeated, as in 740. 9-23, where all depends on one *cum*; cf. 298. 19 ff., 744 20 ff., and many more; clauses simply linked together without any subordination, or without any indication of the beginning of the apodosis, as 407. 22, 528 23, 539. 9, 544. 15, 606. 13, 772. 18, &c.; double relative clauses, as 589. 10, 643. 9, 699. 13; double conditional clauses, as 754. 12, 781. 11; the use of a participle for a relative or conditional clause, as 499. 23, 518. 14, 687. 11; the use of the genitive and ablative in many eccentric senses, and other causes which can only be dealt with in a discussion of syntax. Such grammatical peculiarities as seem to be rhetorically intended are mentioned later. Beside these must be named the omission of words or prefixes through a cognate preceding as 600. 22 *in tanto fratrum religiosoque conuentu* (i. e. *tam religioso*), 628. 7 *pari grauitate et salubri moderatione* (i. e. *pariter salubri*), so perhaps also 671. 19 *talia ac tanta et multa exempla* (i. e. *tam multa*) should be read. With these may be compared ps -Apul. *Ascl.* 8 (33. 24 Goldb.) *tantus et bonus,* Hieron *Ep.* 48. 12 *toties et crebro.* The prefix *con-* is omitted 431. 23 *conluetare et gratulare melioribus,* 701. 2 *collegarum et sacerdotum*; cf. Apul. *Apol.* 40 (51 15 Kr.) *conexa et catenata.* Correlatives also are omitted occasionally, as 189 17, 383. 24. Cyprian's mistakes usually occur near the end of his writings, and are especially common in the long controversial letters, of which he seems to have grown tired before they were finished.

most rarely, to be found in Cyprian, whose own favourite words, e.g. *blandiri, copulare, cumulare, grassari, magisterium, obsequium, proficere, repraesentare*, are in no wise frequent in Tertullian. The only writing of Cyprian's which seems to show signs of his master's influence in style is *Ep.* 63, certainly one of his earliest compositions. It contains such words as *taxare* and *laetificare* (705. 19, 710. 18), which he afterwards avoids. Yet a fair proportion of the few needless Greek words employed are loans from Tertullian; cf. p. 296.

The influence of Minucius Felix on Cyprian, or rather the wholesale borrowing from him in the *Ad Don.*, and the more moderate loans elsewhere (e. g. *B. Pat.* § 3, which contains *qui non loquimur magna sed uiuimus* (398. 21) from Min. Fel. 38. 6, which in its turn probably comes from Sen. *Ep.* 26. 5 *utrum loquar fortia an sentiam*) is so obvious and well indicated already that it need not be retailed here. Their style also is very similar [1].

§ 5. Cyprian's object in such treatises as the *De Habitu Virginum* and *De Patientia* was no doubt to give his people the benefit of Tertullian's thoughts, while providing a substitute for writings which, however harmless themselves, would probably lead their readers on to Montanist works of the same author. A similar motive seems to have led Cyprian to compose the *Ad Donatum*. The philosophical writings of Apuleius, composed in that ornate style which was as pleasing to Cyprian's age as to himself, must have been a dangerous attraction to the less convinced Christians. In all probability they were written with a deliberate religious purpose; perhaps even the *Metamorphoses* were composed by Apuleius in order to attract his readers to the Mysteries, with an ecstatic account of which he ends his book. The *Ad Donatum* appears to be a counterblast to such literature as this, probably to the very writings of Apuleius which are extant. The theory of a definite purpose of presenting Christianity in its most pleasing aspect, as a mystery initiation into which brings new

[1] If evidence be still needed of the earlier date of Minucius, I have given a small proof on p. 225.

life and joy, and presenting it vaguely, without revelation of its inward teaching, but with all the attractions of what passed for the highest eloquence, seems a better account of the work than the supposition usually entertained, that it is the crude and florid production of a new and ill-instructed convert. No stress need be laid upon the apparent autobiography which it contains; a neophyte in his first enthusiasm is the natural speaker in such a composition. It is a piece of literary workmanship, and only in that light can it be judged. Its style is no evidence that it was written soon after Cyprian's conversion. He was emphatically a man of his day, and his generation regarded such writing with admiration. Tertullian had already set the example of a Christian teacher indulging in rhetorical display, and that without any excuse of possible usefulness. The *de Pallio*, with its elaborate antitheses and assonances and all the artificial graces of the time, its *minimum* of Christianity and its adulation of the Severi, is as clearly written for the sake of words as Fronto's praises of Smoke and Dust or anything in the *Florida* of Apuleius. Cyprian had at least a serious subject, if he treated it somewhat trivially. At any moment during his episcopate the need for a rhetorical antidote to rhetorical pagan tracts may have arisen, and when the need arose his education enabled him to supply it. That his standard of taste did not change is shown by *Ep.* 76, which contains some of his most highly coloured rhetoric, written under the inspiration of approaching martyrdom within a few weeks of his death [1]. That such an indirect reply to pleas for paganism might naturally be made is shown, I think, conclusively by the *Asclepius* attributed to Apuleius. Unless I am entirely mistaken, that piece is translated from the Greek by a deliberate imitator of the writings of Cyprian. Cyprian found it necessary to show the world that Christian

---

[1] Against this view of the *Ad Don.* must be set Augustine's statement that it was his work as a new convert. *Doctr. Chr.* 4. 14. This, at any rate, has been the view usually taken of Augustine's meaning. But does he necessarily imply more than that *Ad Don.* stood at the beginning of his copy?

literature could be as attractive as heathen; a generation later the literary advantage was on the side of Christianity.

It would be impossible to show any direct influence of Apuleius on Cyprian, though nothing can be clearer than the fact that both had been trained in the same school of rhetoric. The writers on the style of Apuleius might, with a very small amount of change, turn their books into treatises on Cyprian. There is only one of Apuleius' devices, the use of diminutives, which is not also employed by Cyprian[1]. Apuleius, a leisurely writer aiming at nothing but effect, uses his tricks of style with much more frequency than Cyprian; yet Cyprian has them always at command, and on occasion, as in the *Ad Don.*, the perorations of most of his treatises and the panegyrical letters, can use them as lavishly as Apuleius himself[2]. The symmetrical arrangement of balanced clauses, the constant pleonasm (for Cyprian when striving to be eloquent will always use two words in preference to one), the alliteration, the rhyme, the poetical diction, the forced metaphors and combinations of incongruous words, and all the artifices of style are to be found in both[3]. Though this paper is confined

---

[1] *Clausula* 287. 5 and *summula* 479. 2, 701. 6 are Cyprian's only diminutives of the first declension, and they are not employed for mere effect. *Morula*, 500. 11, is not Cyprian's own, but quoted by him from the words of the recipient of a vision. Diminutives in *-culum* are fairly numerous, but only *conuenticulum* 220. 23, 683. 6 and *corpusculum* 201. 4, 761. 5 are diminutive in more than form.

[2] Kretzschmann, *De latinitate L. Apuleii*, Königsberg, 1865, p. 9 notes the excessive symmetry of Apuleius, *uix autem dici potest quam creber ac nimius fuerit Apuleius in omnibus his dictionis flosculis* (πάρισα, &c.) *studiose appetendis*. Kretzschmann, Becker and Koziol on Apuleius are all useful to a reader of Cyprian, if only to teach him the wide use of pleonasm in this school, and to recognize the superabundance of synonyms without trying to torture them into differences of meaning.

[3] Apuleius' quaint rhyme with adverbs in *-atim*, *Met.* 8. 15 (144. 14 Eyss.) *non laciniatim disperso sed cuneatim stipato commeatu* has an exact parallel in Cyprian 598. 21 *ostiatim per multorum domos uel oppidatim per quasdam ciuitates discurrentes*, where Cyprian has an assonance as well, and so excels his rival. What could be more Cyprianic than *Met.* 4. 19 (68. 4 Eyss.) *his omnibus salubri consilio recte dispositis*? Yet it refers to the arrangements for a burglary.

to one writer, it may be suggested that a comparison of the style of different authors with the text-books of rhetoric would cast much light on the history of education under the Empire, and might be a more certain guide to localization than the study of words, which has been pursued so vigorously of late.

§ 6. Apuleius is not the model of Cyprian; they were only trained in the same school, whatever it may have been; it was, at any rate, not that of Fronto. But Cyprian owes a direct debt to Seneca. In the next chapter (p. 291) one striking metaphor, that of the gladiator for the Christian, has been pointed out as common to both. This is only one of several thoughts which Cyprian owes to the Stoic philosophy of Seneca. As illustrations of hardship the Stoic often dilates on torture, the *eculeus*, the *laminae*, the *frons inscripta*, the wild beasts, &c., dangers which were much more real to the Christian. Hence not only the general sense of Seneca, but even turns of language are reproduced; Sen. *Dial.* 1. 4. 11, *uulnera praebere uulneribus* (Cypr. 491. 17 *torquerentur . . . iam non membra sed uulnera*; for the thought cf. *Mart. Polyc.* 12), *Ep.* 66. 18 *nihil interesse utrum aliquis in gaudio sit an in eculeo iaceat ac tortorem lasset*, *Ep.* 71. 5 *si uirtutem adamaueris quidquid illa contigerit tibi . . . faustum felixque erit ; et torqueri si modo iacueris ipso torquente securior* sq.: *Dial.* 5. 3. 6, *Ep.* 14, 5, &c. (cf. Cypr. 192. 9, 491. 13, 582. 19, &c.). But Cyprian borrows from Seneca on other themes also, and his words as well as his thoughts; *Ep.* 94. 56 *properantis mundi uolubilem cursum* = Cypr. 577. 8 *reuertentis anni uolubilem circulum*, *Dial.* 5. 1. 5 *accessus lenes et incrementa fallentia*, cf. Cypr. 209. 13, 247. 26, &c., *Ep.* 83. 27 *retinere rectum tenorem* = 621. 17, 725. 9, *Dial.* 5. 1. 4 *ira praecipitat* = 225. 11 (cf. 5. 20), though this may be Virgilian, *Aen.* 2. 317; words frequent in both and similarly used are *aestuare, fluctuare, inflari, inconcussus, proficere* (of moral progress), *repraesentare*. The *Ad Don.* especially is full of reminiscences of Seneca[1].

---

[1] Cf. with 8. 25 *aruinae toris* sq. Sen. *Ep* 15. 2; with 9. 1 *carius perire*,

The only other prose writer whom Cyprian evidently knew is Cicero. Though no educated writer of post-Augustan date could fail to show the influence of Cicero, yet there can be none who is less indebted to him than Cyprian. In *Ad Don.* 1 (3. 13) *dum erratici palmitum lapsus . . . repunt* there is an imitation of *De Senectute* 52, *uitis serpens multiplici lapsu et erratico*; and 668. 15 sq. suggests *contempsi Catilinae gladios*. Beside these there seem to be only little expressions which might naturally cling to the memory, such as *turbo et tempestas* 210. 17, 618. 2, *praepropera festinatio* 717. 11, *expugnator matrimonii alieni* 644. 10. Two of Cicero's words, *ingressio* 193. 15, and *impugnatio* (six times: see Hartel's index), seem to have been revived by Cyprian, after an intervening period of neglect.

§ 7. Among existing poets one cannot be sure that Cyprian knew any but Virgil. Lucretius, whom Tertullian and Lactantius know well, Arnobius too well, is never copied. *Arborei fetus* 353. 2 from *Georg.* 1. 55, *frondea tecta* 3. 14 from *Georg.* 4. 61, *furiata mens* 424. 11 from *Aen.* 2. 407, *fluctuans uario mentis aestu* 239. 13 (and 300. 16) from *Aen.* 4. 532, *libat licet gemma* 13. 24 from *Georg.* 2. 506, *fanda atque infanda* 630. 17 from *Aen.* 1. 543, &c., and, most clearly of all, 367. 24 *quando et in agro inter cultas et fertiles segetes lolium et auena dominetur* (alluded to again 385. 9) from *Georg.* 1. 154 *interque nitentia culta Infelix lolium et steriles dominantur auenae*; probably also 577. 14 *per uicissitudines mensium transmeauit hibernum* from *Aen.* 1. 266 *ternaque transierint Rutulis hiberna subactis* (cf. p. 305, n.) are evidences that Cyprian could quote his Virgil, while 4. 8 *exilis ingenii angusta mediocritas . . . nullis ad copiam fecundi caespitis culminibus ingrauescit* from *Ecl.* 1. 68 *congestum caespite culmen* proves that he could forget or mistake his meaning. *Area fruges terit* 304. 24 recalls Tibullus 1. 5, 22 *area dum messes sole calente teret*.

Ep. 115. 8 *carius inepti*. *Ad Don.* § 12 suggests Sen. *Ep.* 115. 8 ff. and *Dial.* 1. 3, 10 ff. But cf. especially *Ad Don.* § 10 (and *Ad Dem.* §§ 10, 11) with *Dial.* 4. 7. 3, and 4. 8. 2.

204 *The Style and Language of St. Cyprian.*

But it is probable that there are also citations from Seneca's tragedies. Their language, of course, has many resemblances to that of the moral writings, and also to prose rhetoric of Cyprian's school. In no play is this so strong as in the *Hercules Oetaeus*. But 355. 23 *si terra situ pulueris squaleat* is very possibly from *Phaedr.* 471 *orbis iacebit squalido turpis situ*; cf. 830. 2 *squalent membra . . . situ et sorde deformia*, which suggests a dislocated hexameter. *Viuax flamma* 368. 16 occurs in *Med.* 826, *compage rupta* 491. 16, though in a different sense, in *Oed.* 580 (plural *Herc. Oet.* 1135, 1228) and *obductae fores* 10. 25 *Herc. Oet.* 1548. These also may be reminiscences.

There are at least two more instances of apparently hexameter lines, from unknown poets, cited indirectly; 353. 10 *nouella ac uegeta iuuenta pollere*, which suggests *uegeta pollere iuuenta*; cf. *auena dominetur* already cited, and 646. 23 *carinam praeualidis et electis roboribus intexe*, which may be from *roboribus ualidis intexe carinam*, and also one iambic *senarius* with its two last words transposed, 474. 7 *nemo diu tutus est periculo proximus*[1].

Beside these instances of actual verse, Cyprian's diction is at least as full of poetical elements as that of any post-Augustan writer. Taking only a few illustrations, and those confined to nouns, *acies* = 'warfare' 495. 6, 526. 15, 654. 9, 663. 23, *clades* 224. 14, 302. 28, &c., *labes* 6. 4, &c., *moles* 15. 10, &c., *sordes* (sing.) 104. 19, 830. 2, *strages* 358. 21, &c., *strues* 13. 20, *suboles* 410. 6, &c., are in form or use poetical, as are *aeuum* = *uita* 6. 3, 364. 20, *aetas* = *tempus* 780. 14, *germen* 189. 12, *gleba* 355. 24, *meta* (of a river) 7. 9, *merx* (sing.) 678. 22, *prex* (sing.) 226. 8, 247. 9, 292. 12, 408. 20, &c., *sudor*

---

[1] No one seems hitherto to have noticed this line. Professor J. E. B. Mayor, who recognizes that it is verse, has pointed out that the thought is in Sen. *Herc. Fur.* 326 f. *nemo se tuto diu Periculis offerre tam crebris potest*, but does not know the line itself. It is not in Wölfflin's *Publilius Syrus*. Jerome, *Ep.* 30. 14 has *nemo, ut beatus Cyprianus ait*, *satis tutus periculo proximus*. Tertullian *Natt.* I. 20 similarly transposes two words of the Hesiodic line to adapt them to prose, — *sic figulus figulo, faber fabro inuidet*.

The Style of St. Cyprian. 205

(of a fountain) 353. 16, *conamina* 687. 15, *lumina* = 'eyes' 8. 24, 10. 26, *pignora* = *liberi* 388. 11, 26, &c.[1] So also with compound expressions: *classicum uocis* 317. 11, *grana pretiosa* = 'jewels' 197. 25 (not in Georges)[2], *durus ac ferreus* 239. 17, *sidus turbidum* 249. 4, *supinae manus* 330. 19, *pauperes uenae* 353. 4, *laborata monilia* 259. 14, *longaeua uita* 353. 25, *crudo tempore* 518. 20, *geminus agon* 580. 4, *candida lux* 230. 11, 369. 24, 577. 13 (also in Apuleius, *Met.* 6. 20, p. 109. 23 Eyss.). *flammis ambientibus medios* 221. 8, *lassa domus* 313. 2, *fons senectute deficiens* 353. 16, *animalia uergente situ ad terram depressa* 362. 16, and many more. The use of simple for compound verbs may also be regarded as poetical, e. g. *forare nauem* 304. 23 = *perforare*, *formare* = *reformare* 402. 12, *premere* = *opprimere* 244. 21, *quaerere* 694. 8, 747. 22, *signare* = *adsignare* 15. 15, *spectare* = *expectare* 539. 11, *sternere* 362. 21, *suadere* = *persuadere* 478. 4, *sumere* = *accipere* 378. 4, 519. 16, and constantly, *tergere* 494. 5, *uertere* 218. 10.

A writer so diffuse as Cyprian could neither use nor originate many proverbial expressions. Otto, in his *Sprichwörter der Römer* and Weyman in his review of that book in Wölfflin's *Archiv*, 8, p. 397, have gleaned what there is; 6. 13 *in proprias laudes odiosa iactatio est*, 13. 27 and 245. 11 *possideri magis quam possidere*, 202. 19 *non est ad magna facilis adscensus*, 419. 10 *de scintillis conflare incendia*, 421. 2 *gladio suo perimi*, 431. 20 *unde uulneratus fueras inde curare*, 505. 12 *parum est adipisci aliquid potuisse, plus est quod adeptus es posse seruare*, 617. 6 *quasi mutasse sit hominem mutare regionem*[3], are the most interesting. To these must be added *nemo diu tutus est periculo proximus* 474. 7, cited above. *Semel uincit qui statim patitur* 577. 3, is perhaps the source of the proverb *uincit qui patitur*[4].

[1] A. Funck in Wölfflin's *Archiv*, 7, p. 101, states that Cyprian is the first to use *pignora* systematically as a substitute for *liberi*.

[2] Cf. Tert. *Res. Carn.* 7 *Rubentis Maris grana candentia*.

[3] This must be simply proverbial, not Horatian. There is no other possible allusion to that poet.

[4] Professor J. E. B. Mayor finds the words imbedded in the *Catonis*

The Style and Language of St. Cyprian.

§ 8. There is no source from which Cyprian draws more freely than his own writings. Phrases, and even long sentences, which he regards as effective are repeated, and this not only in hasty letters written about the same time, but also in his more elaborate productions separated by intervals of years. Felicitous expressions must have been stored up either in his memory or in his common-place book for repetition. One sentence in *Ad Don.* 3 (5. 18 ff.) *necesse est, ut solebat, uinolentia inuitet, inflet superbia, iracundia inflammet, rapacitas inquietet, crudelitas stimulet, ambitio delectet, libido praecipitet,* the alliterations and rhymes of which pleased him, is repeated with modifications in *Un.* 16, and *Mort.* 4 (225. 9, 299. 18), and reminiscences of it are found in *Dem.* 10 and *Z. L.* 6 (357. 27, 423. 6); so with *sol radiat* sq. in *Don.* 14 and *Op.* 25 (15. 11, 393. 27). The very effective conclusion of the *De Opere et Eleemosynis, in pace uincentibus coronam caudulam pro operibus dabit, in persecutione pro passione geminabit,* is repeated from the end of *Ep.* 10, and the thought occurs again 577. 16. Other instances are 241. 1 *negotiationis quaestuosae nundinas aucupari* = 515. 22; 239. 11 *auulsam uiscerum nostrorum partem* = 521. 12; 14. 20 *adridet ut saeuiat* sq. = 202. 14; 13. 13 *caducis uotis* sq. = 390. 20 ff.; 35. 10 *libellus compendio breuiante digestus* = 224. 2, where the sense is quite different; 101. 12 *praeceptorum grande compendium* = 287. 25; 214. 5 *fons ... exundare ... diffundi* = 353. 15, 411. 22, and cf. 642. 15; 301. 22 *imbrem nubila serena suspendunt* = 352. 9; 351. 2 *oblatrantem te ... et obstrepentem,* cf. 229. 13 and 602. 3 (Tert. *adu. Marc.* 2. 5 *init. O canes ... latrantes in Deum ueritatis*). Many more instances might be given[1].

Monosticha (Riese, *Anthol. Lat.* 716. 42), *qui uinci sese patitur pro tempore uincit,* but does not know the source of the usual form. Tert in dilating on the subject in *Apol.* 50 does not put the thought in the form of an aphorism.

[1] I think it might be shown that in some small particulars Cyprian's language varied from time to time; that *adhuc insuper, porro autem, pariter et,* and some other expressions, are only found within certain periods. This might be of use in fixing the date of some of the Treatises, which is not so well ascertained as that of the *Epp.*

The Style of St. Cyprian. 207

§ 9. We may begin our study of the details of Cyprian's style with the rhetorical tropes[1]. Of several of these he makes little use; to others he is devoted. Of metaphorical language, especially, good and bad, his writings are full. Some of it is poetical, some scriptural in origin; perhaps none is very striking. His enemies are *lues*[2] *et pestes* 219. 1, *Patripassiani . . . et ceterae haereticorum pestes et gladii et uenena* 781. 14 (gen. of definition), and similar words are common. Other metaphors are *uarietas uitiorum* 359. 19[3]; *conlidentium uoluntatum diuortium* 215. 8; *animae tinea, cogitationum tabes, pectoris rubigo* 423. 17; *adulteria colorum* 199. 5; *in odium persecutionis facibus liuoris exarsit* 422 5 (cf. 358. 10, 424. 6); *interfector poenitentiae* 694. 4; *nubilum liuoris* 426. 6. Verbs are still more often so employed, e.g. *sopire dolorem*, &c., 685. 9[4], *oblatrantium fluctuum incursus* 667. 24, *domus iam lassa iam fatigata* 313. 2, *effossi et fatigati montes* 353. 3, *calcare carnificinam* 339. 24, *mutilare gloriam*, &c. 238. 23, 794. 10, 841. 11 (cf. *amputare* 425. 16, *castrare* 204. 3), *seminare gloriam*, &c. 577. 19, &c., *destruere castitatem, ueritatem*, &c. 420. 4, and often, *gubernandae ecclesiae libram tenentes* 744. 16, *antiqua illa contra episcopatum meum uenena retinentes* 591. 9, and many more.

Metonymy in Cyprian is almost confined to the use of abstract for concrete nouns (cf. Volkmann, *op. cit.* p. 424 n.), which is carried to an excessive degree; 652. 17 *pacem non deliciis sed armis damus*, 387. 12 *patrimonium copiosum cum indigentium paupertate communicans*, 421. 17 *alta illa sublimitas* (i.e. Satan; cf. *Quod. Id.* 8, p. 25. 14), 190. 18 *quodsi Christum continentia sequitur et regno Dei uirginitas destinatur*, 501. 18

---

[1] As classified by Volkmann, *Rhetorik der Griechen und Römer*, p. 415 ff. Examples could no doubt be given of others than those mentioned, but they would be in no way characteristic of Cyprian's style.

[2] Does this plural occur earlier than Tert. *An.* 30 (350. 11 Reiff.), *Apol.* 20, &c.? Cf. 352. 8.

[3] A medical metaphor; cf. *uarietas leprae* 226. 25, Sen. *N.Q.* 3. 25. 11.

[4] P. Geyer's argument from this word in Wölfflin's *Archiv* 8. 477 is spoiled by his neglect of Cyprian and Arnobius.

208 *The Style and Language of St. Cyprian.*

rogemus . . . cito latebris nostris et periculis subueniri = latentibus et periclitantibus. Mediocritas nostra=ego, 101. 15, &c., is very common (see p. 273); *conscientia uestra* apparently is used for *tu* 656. 16, and elsewhere. Other instances are *cum plebis inaequalitas discreparet* 497. 14, *adunationis nostrae corpus unum* 698. 21, *cum omnium baptismo communicans* 800. 2 and 805. 17, *circumuenire solitudinem singulorum* 693. 1. Abstract periphrases are constantly used for *Deus*, cf. p. 244. Cyprian makes no excessive use of collective abstracts; *fraternitas* is, of course, common; *noua fraternitas*='Cain and Abel' 421. 23, cf. *germanitas Thebanorum, Quod. Id.* 8 (25. 18); *conuiuium=conuiuae* 16. 11, *audientia=auditores* 4. 14, and others[1]. Such abstracts are not only used of persons; 600. 17 *episcopatus tui ordinationem singulorum auribus intimauimus* and the like are very frequent[2].

Here may be classed the use of concrete plurals for abstracts[3]; cf. 357. 13 *delicta mendaciorum, libidinum, fraudium, crudelitatis, impietatis, furoris*, where they are combined with singular abstracts, 510. 2 *gubernacula ecclesiae=gubernatio*, 674. 2 *naufragia*, 728. 4 *mens praua et fallax lingua et odia uenenata et sacrilega mendacia*, and many more. Conversely, plural abstracts in a concrete sense are common: *laudes, uirtutes, gloriae*, as in classical writers.

But Cyprian also frequently changes the meaning of words at his own convenience. *Formido*='object of fear' 209. 10 is classical; but he ventures on *discrimen* for *trutina* 218. 18

---

[1] Cyprian falls far short of other Christian writers; *Vita* 5 (A xcv. 24) *per omnes aditus sollicita caritas circuibat*; Firm. Mat. *Err.* 27. 3 *ut his omnibus* (sc. *typis*) *quasi per gradus quosdam ad lignum crucis salus hominum perueniret = oi σωζόμενοι*; Victor Vit. 1. 25, &c

[2] Abstracts with a genitive are constantly employed; *ueritas* grows quite monotonous, used as it is in 779. 8 *sanctificandi salutaris aquae ueritate*; cf. 223. 16, 305. 13, 341. 11, 379. 23, &c.; so *fides* often, e.g. 660. 9 *fide deuotionis = deuotione fideli*. A characteristic example is 211. 18 *quos detinere non potest in uiae ueteris caecitate circumscribit et decipit noui itineris errore*. Other good instances are 337. 1, 424. 10, 631. 23, 675. 15, 780. 22.

[3] Cf. Wölfflin in his *Archiv*, 5. 492, for instances from *De Aleatt.* So in Hieron. *Ep.* 69. 3 *effusio sanguinis et instar suis in omni caeno libidinis uolutabra = uolutatio*.

(cf. *examen* 528. 4, 665. 7), *simultas* = 'quarrelsomeness' 409. 1, *tenacitas ac firmitas* parallel with *uinculum* and *fundamentum* 407. 26, and conversely *firmamentum* for *firmitas* 489. 10, *conluuio* for *inquinatio* 644. 12, *facinus* for 'guilt' (not 'crime') 679. 20[1]. Instances of verbs with forced and unusual meanings are also common; see *perstringere, praestringere, perstrepere, praestruere* in Hartel's index, *promittere* 493. 10, 594. 4, *proruere* 528. 15. 598. 10, *occurrere* = *succurrere* 523. 19, *subducere* 8. 11, and many more. He delights in devising new shades of meaning, giving a personal subject or object to a verb never so used before, or otherwise showing his ingenuity[2].

Periphrasis is excessively common. Cyprian's devotion to abstract nouns marks his style off from that of the classical writers, and often even impedes his sense, as in 517. 4, 571. 14, 600. 1, 656. 14, 743. 17. *Cremabit addictos ardens semper gehenna et uiuacibus flammis uorax poena* 368. 16, combines pleonasm with periphrasis; cf. *uermium edax poena* = *uermes* 410. 9. Another curious periphrasis is 243. 21 *cui enim non nascenti adque morienti relinquenda quandoque patria?* where *nascens adque moriens* is put for *mortalis*. A periphrastic use of *circa* is as common in Cyprian as in other late writers, 478. 12, 616. 18, 674. 2, &c.

Hendiadys is not very common except with verbs; *properare et uenire* = *properanter* 509. 13, *cum ad me litteras direxerint et petierint* = *petentes* 519. 14, *cum manna deflueret et ... ostenderet* 763. 14, and the like. The substantives come rather under the head of amplification or extension of meaning, as 402. 8 *crudelitas necis et effusio sanguinis*, 259. 15 *indumenta peregrina et sericas uestes*, 577. 6, 710. 14, &c., many of which are cited in § 19.

---

[1] *Facinus* represents ἀνομία in Mt. 24. 12 in Cyprian's Bible, 335. 18; Vulg. *iniquitas*. Jerome has only allowed the word to survive in three cases in the Vulgate; all of these are in the usual sense.

[2] So with adjectives; *succincta diligentia* 101. 9, *delicata congressio* 202. 17, and others which normally would be used of persons, not of abstractions.

210 The Style and Language of St. Cyprian.

Of hyperbaton there is one remarkable form, found also in Apuleius [1], by which one of two co-ordinate words is separated by a copula from those which qualify or agree with it; 524. 2 *incommodo aliquo et infirmitatis periculo = incommodo et periculo infirmitatis*, 603. 1 *supersederunt et ad nos redire noluerunt* [2], 614. 10 *perfidiae et haereticae prauitatis*, 660. 14 *proclamantes et fidem suam per haec uerba testantes*, 518. 16, 538. 4, 670. 17, 768. 22, 795. 4 [3].

Cyprian often displaces his words, sometimes with awkward results, though there can be no doubt that he does it deliberately. Dependent words are frequently pushed to the front, as in the very clumsy instance, 627. 13 *secundum quod tamen ante fuerat destinatum, persecutione sopita cum data esset facultas in unum conueniendi, copiosus episcoporum numerus* [4] sq.; cf. 740. 3 *obrepere autem si hominibus Basilides potuit, Deo non potest*, which may be excused by epiploce with the preceding *obrepsit*, 368. 20, 404. 24, 411. 4, 789. 14 (where *et qui = qui et*), &c. *Esse* especially is often prefixed; 387. 21 *quo amplior fuerit pignorum copia esse et operum debet maior inpensa*, 5. 15, 398. 23, 623. 4, &c. In 243. 21 obscurity is caused not only by a strange periphrasis but by the putting of *non* before its natural place; cf. 514. 16. *Quid* clauses are usually dislocated; 200. 1 *uiderint quid sibi nuptae blandiantur*

---

[1] *Met.* 6. 31 (116. 16 Eyss.) *ultra modum delictique saeuire terminum = modum terminumque delicti*; *Plat.* 1. 15 (77. 7 Goldb.) *pulmones loco ac sui genere cordi plurimum consulunt = loco ac genere*; and perhaps elsewhere. It is an imitation of such poetical licence as Hor. *Carm.* 3. 4. 11 *ludo fatigatumque somno*, Tibullus 1. 3. 56, &c.

[2] To take this as hyperbaton for *supersederunt et noluerunt redire* seems more reasonable than with Hartel (Preface, p. liii) to appeal to an unattested statement of Nonius that the verb *supersedere* may mean 'to be obstinate.' Rönsch, *Beitr.* 3, p. 80 agrees with Hartel.

[3] So also in other writers among Cyprian's *Epp.* In 552. 8 (Novatian) the MSS. read *tenorem euangelici uigoris inlibatam dignitatem seruare.* Hartel reads *tenore*, but *tenorem et* is at least as near to the MSS., and quite possible according to this idiom. So Cornelius (613. 15) *malitia et inexplebili auaritia*, and Nemesianus (835. 3) where, for the MS. *ut . . . cadauera* (or *cadaueris*) *ipsius publici hostis nerui concisi calcarentur, cadauer et* should probably be read, instead of *et* being inserted after *hostis*, as by Hartel.

[4] This separation by a genitive of noun and adjective is rare in Cyprian.

sq., 209. 4, 299. 10, 373. 18, &c.; cf. the extraordinary *quae cum uiris adque uiros* sq., 200. 25. *Prius longe quam* 498. 18, *multum malitia protracta* 399. 18 (cf. 424. 22), and the like, occasionally occur.

Adverbs and conjunctions are often put unnaturally late in the sentence. *Namque* is third 651. 17, 735. 23, *etenim* third 771. 8, *utique* fourth 727. 12. *Et* also is often displaced, occurring once in the sixth place, 698. 21. Such arrangements as 264. 8 *quam contristauerat nuper laetam faciet ecclesiam*, 318. 13 *si confectam et paratam iam uestem darem*, 507. 23 *post confessionem sanctificata et inlustrata plus membra*, 578. 21 *in carne adhuc licet uobis positis*, are common[1].

§ 10. Cyprian does not furnish many examples of playing upon language. Verbs are sometimes used in two senses; e.g. 383. 17 *seruas pecuniam quae te seruata non seruat*, 403. 5 *si admissum facinus agnoscant . . . ad praemium regni caelestis admittit*, 466. 4 *sed aliis terram colentibus illa* (sc. *leuitica tribus*) *tantum Deum coleret*, 688. 21 *ut . . . magis petant fundi pro se preces adque orationes antistitis quam ipsi fundant sanguinem sacerdotis*, 711. 12 *nos omnes portabat Christus qui et peccata nostra portabat*[2]. So with substantives; 402. 14 *ut . . . palmis in faciem uerberaretur qui palmas ueras uincentibus tribuit*; cf. 724. 18 *si uero apud insanos furor insanabilis perseuerauerit*, and 616. 10 *Nouatiani et Nouati nouas . . . machinas*, which never recurs, obvious though it is. Perhaps the only instances of oxymoron are *grande conpendium* 110. 12, 287. 25 (cf. Aug. *C. D.* 4. 21 *magnum conpendium*), *magna et diuina breuitas* 288. 1, *fetus sterilis, nubila serena* 301. 20, 22. Cyprian indulges in few conceits; 582. 21 the confessors' feet are bound,

---

[1] Examples of tropical language not so often used by Cyprian are, (1) the proleptic use of adjectives 13. 11, 353. 25, 378. 15, 741. 12; (2) litotes, only in such mild expressions as *non facile = nequaquam* 320. 1, and often, and similarly *minus, minime* and a few more; (3) hyperbole 239. 11 *auulsam uiscerum nostrorum partem* (repeated 521. 12, and perhaps suggested by Hor. *Carm.* 2. 17. 5), 491. 17, 528. 5, 679. 23; (4) brachylogy, such as is classed by Volkmann (p. 423) under synecdoche, 217. 25, 427. 3, &c.

[2] Ordinary zeugma is common enough in Cyprian; 481. 6, 693. 6, &c.

yet they are trampling on the serpent[1] (cf. 619. 6), 710. 21 wine changed to water, 829. 10 gold carried to the mine.

§ 11. Nothing is more characteristic of Cyprian than his striving after symmetry in the formation of his periods. Of parisosis many examples must necessarily be given in illustration of other figures, and therefore few are given here; 313. 25 *qualis illic caelestium regnorum uoluptas sine timore moriendi, et cum aeternitate uiuendi quam summa et perpetua felicitas*, where it is combined with rhyme, antithesis and chiastic arrangement[2], 491. 10 *uidit admirans praesentium multitudo caeleste certamen Dei et spiritale proelium Christi, stetisse seruos eius uoce libera, mente incorrupta, uirtute diuina, telis quidem saecularibus nudos, sed armis fidei credentis armatos*, where there are two short instances of parisosis, *Dei*, *Christi* being inserted to fill out the one, and *credentis* to complete the other, 365. 18 *exultant semper in Domino et laetantur et gaudent in Deo suo, et mala adque aduersa mundi fortiter tolerant, dum bona et prospera futura prospectant*, 740. 1, &c. In the concluding section of *Ad Dem.*, 370. 15-22, there is a succession of six groups of clauses, arranged by two, three and four, of nearly equal length[3]. Indeed, Cyprian constantly for the purpose of balance inserts otiose words; many of the instances cited under the head of amplification are due to this desire rather than to a simple preference for two words instead of one; cf. 201. 10 *simul cum amictu uestis honor corporis . . . ponitur*, 311. 11 *uenturus ad Christi sedem, ad regnorum caelestium claritatem lugere non debet et plangere, sed potius secundum pollicitationem Domini, secundum fidem ueri in profectione hac sua et translatione gaudere*, where *secundum fidem ueri*, whatever it may mean[4], is simply inserted to increase

---

[1] Reading *calcatus* instead of *galeatus*; cf. p. 213 n.

[2] Chiasmus is very common, e. g. 198. 22, 204. 17, 390. 22, 694. 3. It is, of course, often combined with other figures, under which examples occur.

[3] This equivalence makes Hartel's conjecture of a lacuna in line 17 unlikely. It is also probable that *patri* was meant to rhyme with *caelesti*, as *crucis* rhymes with *sanguinis* just before.

[4] Cf. *Fragm. Iuris Vat.* § 282; it seems to represent Cyprian's common *fides ueritatis* = *fides uera*.

the number of pairs to four. Other examples are 421. 11, 580. 11, 598. 19 ff., in all of which words appear to be added in order to make one clause equal in length to another.

One of the worst and most constant features of Cyprian's style is the monotonous arrangement of his words in twos and threes. Of the former many instances must be given hereafter under amplification; but even when he is not filling out his sentences with synonyms he is equally careful to save his words from standing alone; cf. 237. 17 *adest militum Christi cors candida qui persecutionis urgentis ferociam turbulentam stabili congressione fugerunt, parati ad patientiam carceris, armati ad tolerantiam mortis*, where four substantives are provided with adjectives, and all is followed by a pair of symmetrical rhyming clauses. These again are followed by three rhyming clauses of equal length. Similarly 364. 7 *per ipsa quae vos cruciant et fatigant probari et corroborari nos scimus et fidimus*, and 682. 14, where, to complete the symmetry, mere pleonasm, such as *poenas aeternas et supplicia perpetua*, is admitted. For other examples of this love of pairs of words see p. 230.

Though it not so easy to arrange words in threes as in pairs, Cyprian very frequently does it. Beside other instances given in this paper, such passages as 493. 3. 523, 4 (where *et confessorum praesentiam*, in form if not in substance, seems due to this desire), 587. 11, 663. 23, 668. 12, 712. 8, are strong evidence for the use even where the reading is somewhat doubtful, as in 582. 22 and 746. 11 [1]. The third co-ordinate word or phrase is often loaded for emphasis; 669. 9 *exaltatio et inflatio et adrogans ac superba iactatio*, 689. 2 *nullus Dei sacerdos*

---

[1] In 582. 22 Hartel reads *et quamuis ligati neruo pedes essent, galeatus serpens et obtritus et uictus est*. But the MS. evidence is strong for *calcatus* and against *galeatus*, which is only read by *P*, *qui plurima coniecturis peringeniosis uerauit* (Hartel, Pref. p. xxxiii). *Calcare* and *obterere* are combined again in 428. 9 and 664. 20. In the last passage is a play upon the words *calciati* and *calcari*; here upon the *ligati pedes*, which yet are free. In 746. 11 *ubi sit tutus accessus et salutaris introitus et statio secura* the evidence is divided, in a badly attested letter, between the insertion and omission of *accessus*. Hartel brackets the word, but in a doubtful case Cyprian's usage is sufficient to turn the scale in its favour, as also in 646. 20.

214 *The Style and Language of St. Cyprian.*

sic infirmus est, sic iacens et abiectus, sic inbecillitate humanae mediocritatis inualulus qui sq., 422. 10 *innocentem, misericordem, miti lenitate patientem*, 243. 16, 390. 21, 505. 24, 681. 14, &c. Even a sixfold combination occurs, as in 687. 19, 730. 10. Many triple rhymes and pleonasms will be found in §§ 14, 16

Cyprian's range of subjects naturally led him often to contrast truth with error; but the opportunities for symmetrical arrangement which antithesis gives had perhaps quite as much to do with his devotion to that figure. Antithesis real and unreal, combined usually with parisosis or other figures, abounds in his pages. *Ep.* 38, especially, contains little else. Such strings as 806. 5 *succumbat et cedat ecclesia haereticis, lux tenebris, fides perfidiae, spes desperationi, ratio errori, immortalitas morti, caritas odio, ueritas mendacio, Christus antichristo*, are very common; cf. *Fort.* 6 *tit.*, 593. 18, 687. 19. 773. 5, &c.

This love of symmetry is clearly manifested in numerous abrupt changes of voice in the verbs. In order to gain apparent uniformity the subject is violently altered and a passive introduced in the second half of a sentence, the first half of which has had a deponent verb; e.g. 402. 24 ff. *ille non loquitur nec mouetur nec maiestatem suam sub ipsa saltim passione profitetur; usque ad finem perseueranter ac iugiter tolerantur omnia ut consummetur in Christo plena et perfecta patientia*, 410. 13 ff., 423. 10 ff., &c. Conversely, the first clause is made to adjust itself to the second, 276. 24, &c.

§ 12. Certain grammatical devices are also freely used for rhetorical purposes. One of the most frequent is the use of plural abstracts, which is also characteristic of Apuleius (Koziol, p. 251). Instances are *acerbationes* 600. 21, *administrationes* 629. 9, *anxietates* 405. 16, *confessiones* 481. 3, *conflictationes* 299. 11, and often, *conluctationes* 405. 23, *conspectus* 237. 15, *dignationes* (acts of favour) 500. 13, &c., *infestationes* 406. 4, 501. 11, *meditationes* 430. 14, *miserationes* 379. 24 (also Bibl.), *postulationes* 319. 12, *tarditates* 318. 25, *ultiones* 363. 8, 366. 10 (Bibl.).

Here may also be placed the use of verbal nouns as attributes, which is very common, e.g. *desertor adsecla* 13. 11, *expugnator inimicus* 201. 18 (where *inimicus* is the substantive, cf. *subtilis inimicus* 249. 10). *inpium et persecutorem (fratrem)* 404. 8, and especially *peccator*, as *peccator populus* 273. 25, cf. 641. 7, 670. 5, 769. 2, &c. Cyprian extends this attributive use to substantives of other forms, as 3. 14 *baiulae arundines*, 13. 7 *comes pompa* (cf. 401. 10), 360. 24 *index uox*, 581. 12 *martyr lector*, 724. 6 *superstes crapula*. In this respect Tertullian (cf. Sittl, *Lokale Verschiedenheiten*, p. 110) far exceeds Cyprian, and Ambrose again leaves Tertullian in the rear [1].

As in other third century writers [2] derivative adjectives constantly take the place of a subjective or objective genitive, and even of a prepositional expression. *Dominicus* and *ecclesiasticus* especially are so used, e. g. 642. 23 *ecclesiasticum corpus*, 621. 5 *litteris ... quas ad me de uestra regressione et de ecclesiastica pace ac fraterna redintegratione fecistis*, where the aim is uniformity, 319. 15, 656. 21, and often *dominica confessio* (by the martyrs), 309. 19 *arcessitio dominica* (cf. *Pass. Perp.* 18 *fin. dominicae passiones*), 390. 1, 699. 15 *nummaria cupiditas, quantitas*, 652. 5 *saturitas dominica* (bestowed by the Lord), 204. 5 *diuinum munus et patrium* = *Dei Patris*, 411. 8 *caput bubulum*, the last being a loan from Tertullian *Jud.* 1.

Present participles, often of verbs which Cyprian uses in no other form, and in senses which cannot be distinguished from those of an adjective, are very common, e. g. *adulantia blandimenta* 247. 11, *angentes fortunae, iniuriae*, &c., 14. 3, 301. 5, 412. 15, 657. 22, 710. 17, *discordans et dissidens* 285. 16,

---

[1] It may be noticed that though Cyprian, like other writers after Livy, uses substantives in *-tor* to express a single act as well as a state or quality (cf. Schmalz, *Stilistik*, § 2 in Iwan-Muller's *Handbuch*), he is very sparing of such use ; 379. 8, 644. 10, 734. 13, and a few more.

[2] E. g. Apuleius, see Koziol, p. 255; cf. Hildebrand's note to Arnobius, p. 449, and Zink on Fulgentius Myth. Other writers on late Latin authors make the same remark. Perhaps Arnobius goes furthest in this direction.

discrepans 602. 7, *exundans* 214. 6, 353. 15, 411. 23, *fallens* 247. 26, 360. 21, 421. 1, *ferociens* 7. 16, 484. 10, 630. 22, *frustrans* 13. 15, 390. 23, *incursans* 8. 5, 356. 25, 625. 6, *lenocinans* 198. 21, *multiplicans* 241. 3, *oblectans* 4. 1; cf. Léonard's Introduction, § 36. Such participles are often joined with an adjective; 407. 1, 507. 2, 629. 3, &c.

The neuter plural of adjectives, with or without a genitive following, is also a favourite usage; *aduersa mundi* 363. 22, 431. 2, *extrema mortis* 724. 16, *secreta et abdita mentis* 383. 13, *arcana cordis atque abdita* 653. 6 (cf. 257. 12, 268. 26, 423. 5, 563. 13 (Roman), Thielmann in Wölfflin's *Archiv*, 3. 490), *occidua* 353. 11, *caelestia = caelum* 204. 4 (for *superna* in the same sense see p. 285), *amatoria* 195. 17, *canora musica* 420. 5 (cf. Apul. *Plat.* 1. 1, 64. 3, Goldbacher), *serena longa* 352. 9, &c.

Cyprian is very moderate in the combination of different degrees of comparison. Superlative is followed by positive in 239. 10 *maximas eximiasque uirtutes*, 313. 26 *quam summa et perpetua felicitas*, 477. 13 *summus et magnus fructus*, 672. 14 *summa et magna*; conversely, 394. 4 *quam grandis et summa laetitia;* superlative by comparative 288. 5 *praecepta prima et maiora,* cf. 339. 2; comparative by positive 191. 11 *meliora et diuina*, 468. 16 *frugaliores et innocentes cibi*. Similar irregularities are 222. 7 *inexpiabilis et grauis culpa*, 293. 17, 504. 17 (cf. 303. 19) *frequenter ac semper*, 576. 9 *satis ac plurimum*, 687. 2 *castra inuicta et fortia*, 754. 16 *quam sine spe sint et perditionem sibi maximam ... adquirant* sq. It will be seen that most of these are legitimate; and it must be remembered that the irregular superlative had practically become positive. Comparative adjectives and adverbs, as in other late writers, are constantly used indefinitely or as equivalent to superlatives. There are nine instances in the short *Ad Don.*; cf. 104. 31, 313. 5, 483. 11, 603. 8, &c.

The Greek attraction of the relative, and the merging of the antecedent in it, is also common. This attempt at conciseness sometimes leads to obscurity, as in 582. 6, where the subject to

The Style of St. Cyprian. 217

cui plus licuit et coegit is *ecclesia* [1], the *et* marking the apodosis; cf. 282. 7, 287. 15, 306. 2, 386. 18, &c. *Secundum quod* is especially common in citations, 285. 17, &c. Hartel's Index is far from exhausting the instances.

Certain other usages are adopted for rhetorical purposes, especially the historical infinitive, which is found five times, 6. 6, 217. 20, 240. 21, 242. 14, 255. 12. Among these are both descriptive and narrative passages. The employment also of *ut* clauses in many and often strange senses [2], consecutive, explanatory or other, as 195. 23, 569. 13, 678. 12, &c., of *quod* clauses as 320. 17 *ne . . . perdant quod euaserint* (repeated 501. 2), 664. 1 *ne perdat integer quod nuper stetit*, 202. 22, 298. 18, 403. 25, &c., in some of which *quod* may be a relative and object to the verb, as in 769. 14 *consentire in id quod illi baptizauerint* [3], seems often to be dictated by rhetorical motives.

Hypallage, sometimes bold enough, is not uncommon. Instances are 202. 26 *magna uos merces habet*, 576. 12 *uestris cordibus adhaeremus* = 'you love us,' 716. 6 *quod furtum et adulterium ne in nos etiam cadat cauere sollicite . . . debemus*, 195. 8 *patrimonio tuo Deum faenera* (repeated 263. 8, 386. 11), 584. 25 *presbyterii honorem designasse nos illis sciatis*, 682. 5 *exarmatur fides militantis populi*.

§ 13. Nothing shows the rhetorical training of Cyprian better than his use of rhythm, rhyme, and alliteration. Rhythm, even more than the others, displays this. In this respect the *Ad Donatum*, Cyprian's most rhetorical writing, shows just the same results on examination as his other Treatises and the Letters. Taking the ends of periods (including in them the words preceding a colon) we find that six forms all but exhaust the list. There are 150 of these

---

[1] The period should surely be placed after *suadentibus*. *Nobis suadentibus cui plus licuit* for 'the Church which had greater rights over him than I who was urging him' is not only harsh but unlike Cyprian.

[2] Though not often final; *ad hoc . . . ut* or some further definition is usual.

[3] Cf. Ambr. *Ep.* 63. 9 *perdiderunt utique quod ieiunauerunt, perdiderunt quod se aliquo continuerunt tempore*.

terminations. Of these fifty-five are of the form $\cup\cup \cup \mid - - \cup$ (*tecta fecerunt, gerere festinant, amoena consentit*, &c.), and forty-five are trisyllabic in their ending, nine terminate with a monosyllable followed by a word of two syllables (*ex nobis, hanc sedem*, &c.), and one with three monosyllables (*usus est, ars est*)[1]. A tribrach is only used five times before the final trisyllable; the usual trochee is much more often a whole word than a termination. The next terminal rhythm in number is $- \cup - \cup$, of which there are twenty-seven instances, only four of which are vitiated by a long syllable at the end. Twenty are formed by one word (*sortiatur*, &c.), six by two words, the first a monosyllable (*et fauebam* 6. 2, where the *et* is put out of place for the purpose, *non timetur*, &c.), only two by dissyllables (*saepe mecum*). Then follows $- \cup - \mid - \cup \cup$ with twenty-two examples (*amore quo diligis, conuiuium sobrium*), of which seven have the last syllable long, and two the first resolved into two short (*indicia praenoscimus, adsidua uel lectio*). Twelve have a trisyllabic word at the end, five one of four syllables (*poenitenda contagia*, &c.), and the rest two words (*iura proscripta sint, singuli crimen est*, &c.). Then comes $- \cup \mid \cup \cup - \cup$, that *esse uideatur* ending which Quintilian (9. 4. 73, 10. 2. 18) complains of as hackneyed. Of these there are fourteen, all but one (*damnare quod eramus*) ending in a four-syllabled word, and only one (*donantur alieni*) having its final syllable long. Then comes $- \cup \mid - \cup \cup \cup$ (*ueritate simplicia, pectus et pateat*, &c.) with twelve instances, eight ending in a four-syllabled word, and five with a long syllable, and finally twelve of $\cup - - \cup$ (*reuelabo, recensere, facit mecum, pauor nullus*, &c.) with five examples of a word of four syllables, five with two words, and one (*elaboratam*) extending beyond the termination. The six terminations account for 137 of the 150 cases, in 105 of which the last word is of the quantitative value of $- - \cup$ at least. Only thirteen cannot be accounted for under these six heads.

---

[1] For two monosyllables regarded as equivalent to a dissyllable cf. Bahrens' Preface to *Poetae Latini Minores*, vol. I, p. xii.

The Style of St. Cyprian.

In the *De Lapsis*, not quite so carefully written, out of 262 endings all but twenty-eight fall under the same six heads. Nearly a third, eighty-one, are of the form $\stackrel{\smile}{-} \cup \mid -- \stackrel{\smile}{-}$, sixty of $- \cup - \cup$, twenty-eight of $- \cup - \mid - \cup \stackrel{\smile}{-}$, twenty of $- \cup \mid \cup \cup - \cup$, sixteen of $- \cup \mid - \cup \cup \stackrel{\smile}{-}$, and twenty-nine of $\cup -- \cup$[1].

In the *De Bono Patientiae*, more carefully written than the *De Lapsis*, of 123 terminations all but seventeen come under the above heads; thirty-two under the first, twenty-five under the second, fourteen (of which seven are of the resolved form $- \cup \cup \cup \mid - \cup \stackrel{\smile}{-}$ as *uera patientia, fecit in origine*) under the third, thirteen under the fourth, nine under the fifth, and thirteen under the last. Of the remaining seventeen, seven are of a form rare in *Ad Don.* and *De Lapsis*, that of $- \cup - \mid --$, as *actibus nostris, benignius dici*.

Taking next six of the most rhetorical Epistles, 10, 28, 37, 38, 39, 58, together, the result is found to be much the same. Of 192 terminations all but twenty come under the six heads, the numbers belonging to which are respectively 56, 40, 23 (four in the resolved form), 16, 7, and 30.

It may be sufficient to take two more letters, both long ones, *Ep.* 59 to Cornelius, denouncing Novatian's party, and the controversial *Ep.* 73 to Jubaianus on Baptism. In the former, which contains 118 terminations, the numbers of the

---

[1] It will be seen that there are comparatively few of the more difficult forms. Of the first form, twenty-eight are of two complete words, as *mundus eluxit* and forty-three have the first word longer. In ten the first is, or ends with, a tribrach. In eight two words (*iacere me credo*, &c.) are employed to form the final molossus. Two are formed of one word, *nuntiauerunt, praedicauerunt*, and in one, *et rogauerunt* (242. 17), the *et* is put out of its place to secure this ending. Of the second form forty-two are words of four syllables (fifteen with the final long), sixteen have a monosyllable first (*ut periret*, &c.) and two are of two dissyllables. Of the third form sixteen end with four-syllabled words; the others are of three or compound tenses; there should be added one of the form $- \cup \mid \cup \cup - \cup \cup$ (*sponte properauimus*). Of the *esse uideatur* form all end with words of four syllables. Of the fifth form all except three ending with three-syllabled words (*communicare se simulant*, &c.) end with words of four. Of the twenty-nine of the last form, twenty-two are of four syllables and seven of two dissyllabic words; seven have the final long.

220 The Style and Language of St. Cyprian.

different forms are 22, 28, 18, 5, 11, 11. These with seven of – ⏑ – | – –, mentioned as also fairly numerous in *De B. Pat.*, and sixteen irregular, make up the whole number. In *Ep.* 73, written, like all those on the same subject, with less regard to form than Cyprian's other works, the numbers among 123 terminations are 23, 22, 18, 8, 7, 15. Among the large proportion of thirty exceptions are many of four long syllables (*baptizari*, &c.), which hardly occur in those previously analyzed[1].

Little would be gained by going through more of Cyprian's writings[2]; the results would be the same. He had no doubt been trained so effectually that his sentences, however hastily written, instinctively ended with one of the forms already mentioned. Very rarely does he end with a short word, except when two combine to form one of these terminations; hardly ever is there a hexametrical ending.

Cyprian's care for rhythmical endings can clearly be seen in the varying forms of such words as *contagium* with its alternative *contagio*. The former, which is the normal form of the third century, is used twenty-four times, the latter fourteen times, often demonstrably, as in 203. 14 *contagione transitis* and 829. 15 *contagione maculetur*, to produce a rhythmical effect which the other would not have given. A more remarkable instance is *saepe*. *Frequenter* is the normal word for 'often' throughout Cyprian; *saepe* is never used except for rhythm[4], terminal or other, and is comparatively rare.

---

[1] Without going through the particulars as fully as in *Ad Don.* and *De Laps.* it may be mentioned that in *De Pat.* the terminations are unusually harmonious and perfect. The same may be said of the six rhetorical letters. Among other signs of Cyprian's comparative indifference to the styles of *Epp.* 58 and 73, and others like them, is the rarity of the *esse uideatur* ending, and the greater number (in *Ep.* 73 nearly 25 per cent.) of irregular endings.

[2] Yet an occasional emendation might result, as in 779. 2, where *quaerente rescripserim*, for which there is some authority, is much more in Cyprian's style than the better attested *quaerenti* of Hartel's text, and in 483. 10, 633. 14, 711. 22, where *perseuerent, multa diuersitas, dilectio* should be read.

[4] 5. 21, 251. 4, 260. 13, 422. 10, 435. 14, 475. 21, 569. 19, 576. 8, 629. 10, 764 16, 765. 9, and perhaps a few more times.

The Style of St. Cyprian. 221

The solitary instance of *fateri* for *confiteri* is due to rhythm, *ut ... Christum uictrix lingua fateatur* 665. 1[1]. All these Cyprianic terminations are usual enough in classical writers, and are among those approved by Quintilian, 9. 4. 93 ff.[2]

§ 14. Rhyme, though only of a few types, is common in Cyprian. Within the same clause such rhymes as 405. 12 *cum sudore et labore*, 593. 7 *amore et ardore*, 793. 4 *pudorem eius et honorem*, 602. 13 *nouitate uel prauitate*, 229. 26 *sanctitas et dignitas*, 320. 11 *diuitias et delicias*, 693. 7 *malitia et saeuitia*[3], 314. 2 *gloriam et uictoriam*, 742. 4 *nec annis nec minis*, 248. 16 *contumacibus et peruicacibus*, 748. 4 *execrabiles et detestabiles*, 765. 7 *laudabiles ac probabiles*, 420. 11 *exerte adque aperte*, are frequent[4]; cf. 6. 14 *quamuis non iactatum possit esse sed gratum*, 255. 22 *tanta est potestas Domini, tanta maiestas*, 267. 3 *fundamenta aedificandae spei, firmamenta conroborandae fidei*, a good example of parisosis, 390. 22, and many more. It is also combined with other figures; 239. 22 *integritas propria et sanitas priuata*, 664. 3 *integros honor, lapsos dolor ad praemium prouocet*. Longer examples often occur, as 204. 17 *hanc imaginem uirginitas portat, portat integritas, sanctitas portat et ueritas, portant* sq.; in 305. 6 and 749. 9 are three nouns of the same form; cf. 424. 8, 694. 4.

Rhymes at the end of parallel clauses are also common;

---

[1] *Conpago* 231. 10, 642. 24, *conpages* 5. 8, 197. 20, 226. 14, 304. 23, 491. 16, 712. 6, *adfectus, adfectio; consensus, consensio*, and other alternatives may be accounted for in the same way.

[2] In *Gött. Gel. Anz.*, 1893, is an important paper by W. Meyer on rhythm in later Latin. He only makes one incidental mention of Quintilian, appearing to hold that a complete revolution took place in the second century, and that earlier writers need not be taken into account. His examples of quantitative rhythm are taken from Cyprian. The analysis is admirable, but too elaborate and even artificial, making no allowance for exceptions. His theory of the pervading cretic serves well for the grouping of instances; but Cyprian's final cretic is usually a dactyl, and he loves to end with a molossus.

[3] Cf. *malitia et nequitia* 1 Cor. 5. 8 in Cyprian's Bible (125. 16) as well as in the Vulgate.

[4] Similarly in 794. 4 I would read *non putant se alternis immo aeternis peccatis communicare*. The *alienis* of the MSS. is pointless, and *immo* points to a play on words, as in 279. 7.

261. 17 *iniuste sibi placentes et transpunctae mentis alienatione dementes*, 382. 22 *cogitatio . . . meditatio*, 357. 25 *peccatur . . . placeatur*, 370. 18, 390. 26, 432. 14, &c.; cf. 277. 25 *iniuriam facere non nosse et factam posse tolerare*, where *posse* is displaced from the end to get the *esse uideatur* rhythm. In 725. 6 ff. there are three rhymes in one period, *elaborate . . . reuocate . . . consentiant . . . faciant . . . tenorem . . . uigorem*, each ending its clause; and the same number in 706. 13; in 731. 19 there are alternating rhymes, *proscripti sunt . . . fuerunt . . . profecti sunt . . . sumpserunt*.

A word at or near the beginning of a sentence rhyming with another at the end is also frequent; 262. 26 *post indumentum Christi perditum nullum iam uelle uestimentum*, 405. 18 *sudatur enim quamdiu istic uiuitur et laboratur*, 681. 1 *conpelluntur . . . prosecuntur*, 357. 19, 547. 7, 576. 19, 683. 2, &c.

That the number of rhymes of these different kinds is no accident may be seen from the cases in which Cyprian has forced his language into rhyme; 598. 2 *aduentantibus et rei ueritatem reportantibus*, where *aduentare*, a verb most rarely used by Cyprian, is manifestly less appropriate than *aduenire*; 629. 22 *factus est autem Cornelius episcopus de Dei . . . iudicio, de clericorum . . . testimonio, de plebis . . . suffragio, de sacerdotum . . . collegio*, where the last word, which is quite inappropriate, is used for the natural *consensu* (672. 7 and elsewhere) because of its ending, as is *praesentia* for *adsensus* in the similar passage 523. 5; 602. 18 *et laboramus et laborare debemus ut unitatem . . . obtinere curemus* for *obtineamus*; 398. 25 *inde patientia incipit, inde claritas eius et dignitas caput sumit. origo et magnitudo patientiae Deo auctore procedit*, where *et magnitudo* seems inserted because *claritas* in the preceding clause is provided with a rhyme; 731. 17 *Cyprianum . . . sacerdotem Dei agnoscentes et contestantes ei*, where *ei*, a word almost unused by Cyprian, and certainly never placed in an emphatic position elsewhere, is obviously set at the end of the period for rhyme with *Dei*; 394. 28 *in pace uincentibus coronam candidam pro operibus dabit*, *in persecutione purpuream pro passione geminabit* [1], where nothing but the rhyme could have induced him to reject the natural *addet*; 231. 11 *quicquid a matrice discesserit seorsum uiuere et spirare non poterit, substantiam salutis amittit*, where only the rhyme can account for the change of tense; even stronger is 727. 21 *qui iudicio ac testimonio Dei non probantur tantum sed etiam gloriantur.* The sense required is that they receive not mere approval but actual praise. It would be against Cyprian's rules of rhythm to end a period with the hexametrical *glorificantur*; he therefore spoils his sense with *gloriantur*, unless indeed we suppose a verb *gloriare = glorificare*, very rare elsewhere [2]; so also 675. 5 *item Paulus monet nos cum mali de ecclesia pereunt non moueri nec recedentibus perfidis fidem minui*, where the violent change of construction can have no other purpose than rhyme; cf. *erunt ... accipiunt* 252. 14.

Certain imperfect rhymes, which Cyprian appears to have intended for such, may here be mentioned; 302. 28 *cladem, laudem*, 370. 25 *laetus, gratus*, 393. 28 *unus est, communis est*, 471. 10 *locutus est, tuitus est*, 250. 21 *concessum, promissum*, 582. 18 *contabuit, pauit*; cf. *gemino sumus dolore percussi et duplici maerore confusi* in the Roman *Ep.* 36 (572. 12).

It remains to mention that Cyprian carefully avoids parechesis, except in such cases as *bonorum morum*, where it cannot be avoided. There are a few exceptions, as 593. 23 *adulterinis doctrinis*, but very few. One reason for Cyprian's use of *deifica disciplina* may be that *diuina disciplina* breaks this rule; see ch. ii. § 1.

The numerous instances of parallel clauses ending with *est*, *sunt*, &c. are no doubt arranged for purposes of rhyme, e.g. 189. 11 *nunc nobis ad uirgines sermo est, quarum quo sublimior gloria est maior et cura est*, 383. 15 *pecuniae tuae captiuus et seruus es, catenis cupiditatis et uinculis alligatus es, et quem soluerat Christus denuo uinctus es*, 642. 6 *quisquis ille est et qualiscumque*

---

[1] The difference in quantity does not deter Cyprian from this rhyme; *dabit ... inrogabit* occurs 368. 11. *Robore et uigore* is a favourite expression.

[2] Yet cf. *gloriantes* = δοξάζοντες in *Ecclus.* 43. 30.

224 The Style and Language of St. Cyprian.

est, christianus non est qui in Christi ecclesia non est. The number of such terminations is striking; cf. 9. 3 *ut quis possit occidere peritia est, usus est, ars est,* 630. 7 *profanus est, alienus est, foris est.*

§ 15. Alliteration is at least as common as rhyme. The constant use of prepositional prefixes, evidently as much for this purpose as for amplification, is one of the most obvious features of Cyprian's style; e.g. 673. 12 *adplicito et adiuncto,* 802. 8 *addidit et adiecit,* 357. 17 *coartata et conclusa,* 711. 6 *conflueret et conueniret,* 217. 14 *designat et denuntiat,* 353. 5 *decrescit ac deficit,* 639. 5 *disponit et dirigit,* 675. 20 *enitimur et claboramus,* 768. 22 *exorbitans et . . . exerrans,* 357. 14 *increpat et incusat,* 233. 7 *impeditos et inplicitos,* 351. 2 *oblatrantem et . . . obstrepentem,* 632. 18 *offocari . . . et opprimi,* 330. 17 *perseuerandi et permanendi,* 334. 15 *praemonet et praenuntiat,* 772. 9 *praeponere et praeferre,* 213. 9 *renititur et resistit,* 770. 16 *repudiare et reicere,* 687. 4 *suggerit et subministrat.* *Perdere* and *perire* are often combined, 410. 26, 421. 8, &c. Instances in which the alliterative verbs are in parallel clauses, or one of them a participle or replaced by a verbal noun, are also numerous, e.g. 355. 26 *corrumpat . . . consumat,* 368. 6 *adueniens hoc admonet,* 584. 12 *congressioni et paci congruentes;* cf. 356. 6 *ecce uerbera desuper et flagella non desunt.* In these cases the alliterative words are rarely synonyms, but such juxtaposition is far too common to be an accident.

Ordinary alliteration is also very common, especially in the more rhetorical parts of Cyprian's writings; 4. 3 *uoluptaria uisio,* 7. 14 *uenenorum uirus,* 231. 6 *ueri itineris uia* (*uia ueritatis,* &c., 211. 4, 431. 11, 768. 23, 833. 5, and elsewhere), 217. 23 *oris osculum,* 195. 1 *gratia gloriae,* 238. 6 *capita captiua,* 430. 5 *suboles subsecina* ; so also with words connected by conjunctions; 221. 1 *mandauit et monuit,* 373. 2 *multa et magna,* 404. 15 *magna et mira,* 674. 9 *magnalia et mirabilia,* 218. 16 *permittit et patitur,* 393. 13 and 699. 30 *libenter ac largiter,* 229. 25 *firmitas et fides,* 278. 2 *fortiter ac fidenter,* 731. 10 *propria et priuata,* 479. 6 *sollertia et sollicitudo,* 485. 8

credere et crescere, and many more. There are many alliterations also in words balancing one another in the same or different clauses; 3. 12 *dant secessum uicina secreta*, 368. 16 *uiuacibus flammis uorax poena*, 194. 28 *quibus multa magnalia cum miraculo faceret*, 238. 12 *quae cum saeculo sexum quoque uicerunt*, 423. 16 *non hominis sed honoris inimicus*, 577. 22 *hospitium carceris horreum conputatis*, 398. 19 *non uestitu sapientiam sed ueritate praeferimus* [1]; cf. *frugibus ... fraglantia* 352. 28, *uindicta ... uenia* 408. 23. In some cases it is plain that Cyprian has used forced language for purposes of alliteration, as in 582. 7 *nec fas fuerat nec decebat*, where the natural *erat* would not have given the effect, and in 676. 11 *qui non tantum ab his istic abstentus sed et abs te illic ... pulsus est* [2]. So also 279. 7 *cottidianis immo continuis orationibus*, 374. 5 *sanguine et sanctificatione Christi. Cui uita iam deerat uictus abundantiam cogitabat* 282. 7 is an exact parallel to Apuleius, *Flor.* 16. 68 *dolor intestinorum ... conpelleret ante letum abire quam lectum*; yet *uita uictusque* is Ciceronian.

Prolonged alliteration is very common, e.g. 8. 23 *paratur gladiatorius ludus, ut libidinem crudelium luminum sanguis oblectet*, 202. 25 *magna uos merces habet, praemium grande uirtutis, munus maximum castitatis*, 227. 20, 341. 12, 383. 23, 388. 11, 468. 18, &c. Often the alliteration is wholly or in part prepositional; 219. 16 *hos eosdem denuo Dominus denotat et designat dicens me dereliquerunt* sq., 363. 19 *quae de Dei indignatione descendunt*, 497. 12 *in petendo autem fuisse dissonas uoces et dispares uoluntates et uehementer hoc displicuisse illi qui dixerat, petite et inpetratis, quod plebis inaequalitas discreparet* sq., where besides the *dis* alliteration there is another with *u*, 230. 8 ff., &c. In 475. 4 f. a fivefold alliteration with *con-*

[1] This is borrowed from Min. Fel. 38. 6 (54. 20 Halm) *nos qui non habitu sapientiam sed mente praeferimus*, and is evidence, as far as it goes, of the precedence of Minucius. No one, in the third or fourth century, would have altered the alliterative *non uestitu sed ueritate* into the simple equivalent.

[2] The only other instance of *abs* in Cyprian is, I think, 253. 24 *abs te*. For language forced for alliteration cf. 561. 2 (Roman) *si nondum nostrum sanguinem fudimus sed fudisse parati sumus*. The aorist infinitive is simply alliterative.

occurs, ending with the very inappropriate verb *confitetur*; cf. 599. 8, where *confitentur* is chosen because of the preceding *consuluisse*.

Other alliterations are elaborately chiastic; 214. 13 *profluentes largiter riuos latius pandit*, and 732. 8 *Puppianus solus integer inuiolatus sanctus pudicus*, with their arrangements of p. l. r. l. p. and p. s. in. in. s. p., are perfectly symmetrical. Or the alliterative words may begin and end clauses, as 243. 13 *nec ... ad profana contagia sponte properauimus; perdidit nos aliena perfidia; parentes sensimus parricidas,* where an alliteration begins and ends three successive clauses. But such examples are naturally more frequent with kindred words.

§ 16. Parataxis is exceedingly common in Cyprian, and is indeed more characteristic of him than any other rhetorical figure. The simplest form, as 13. 17 *saltibus saltus*, 421. 2 *frater fratris*, 251. 4, 340. 27, 422. 8, &c. is comparatively rare; cf. 254. 21 *ab inmundo spiritu inmunda correpta*, 658. 1 *iusto iustorum praecedentium exemplo*, 357. 19 *indignamini indignari Deum*, &c. Cognate words in close connexion are more common; 199. 22 *quando oculi tibi non sunt quos Deus fecit sed quos diabolus infecit*, 689. 2 *iacens et abiectus*, 690. 11 *nec capi nec decipi*, 657. 14 *uiuit et uiuificat*, 785. 22 (with alliteration) *Paradisi potus salubres et salutares*, 710. 12 *a sapore saeculari resipiscere*, 769. 7 *ut intus per sanctos sanctificetur*, 11. 8, 200. 24, &c. So also when the words are in different, and especially in antithetical, clauses; 362. 23 *cum statu oris et corporis animum tuum statue*, 694. 3 *magis durus saecularis philosophiae prauitate quam sophiae dominicae lenitate pacificus*, where the verbal opportunity has caused Cyprian to overcome his dislike of Greek words, 496. 5 *sibi placentes et omnibus displicentes*, 662. 20 *uenit Antichristus sed superuenit Christus*, 259. 17 *auro te licet ... condecores sine Christi decore deformis es*, 356. 23 *et non agnoscis Dominum Deum tuum cum sic exerceas ipse dominatum?*, 581. 2 *illic fuisse conspicuum gentilium multitudini, hic a fratribus conspici* (so also 357. 26), 428. 18, a double example, *si accepto Spiritu sancto sancte et spiritaliter uiuimus*, cf. 471. 12. Another chiastic instance is 420. 17 *tam paratus semper ad repugnandum quam est ad inpugnandum paratus inimicus.* But Cyprian's favourite instances are *fides* and *sacerdos* with their cognates contrasted with *perfidia, sacrilegium*, &c.; 229. 19 *si . . . fidem primam perfidia posteriore mutauerit*, 769. 12 *dum sacerdotem quaerit in sacrilegum fraude erroris incurrit*, 723. 15 *qui idolis sacrificando sacrilega sacrificia fecerunt sacerdotium Dei sibi uindicare non possunt*, 382. 23, 675. 5, 777. 20, 253. 22, 471. 6, 687. 21, 737. 22, &c.; cf. 226. 5, 431. 1.

But the chief use of this figure in Cyprian is for continuance of thought, not for antithesis. Such language as 277. 20 *qui in aeternum manere uolumus Dei qui aeternus est uoluntatem facere debemus*, 233. 11 *ut . . . euigilet fides nostra uigilantiae praemium de Domino receptura*, cf. the whole passage, 646. 18 *operari tu putas rusticum posse si dixeris 'agrum peritia omni rusticitatis exerce'* sq., where a very rare word has been chosen to keep up the connexion of language, 307. 29, 427. 19, 492. 2, &c. is common. Prolonged parataxis, often combined with anaphora or alliteration, is a marked characteristic of Cyprian's style; 500. 9 *ad . . . dignatione eius indignum . . . mandare dignatus est*, 468. 18 *ceterum quantum uult inde quaerat, qualis quaestus est* sq., 313. 18 *patriam nos nostram paradisum conputamus, parentes patriarchas habere iam coepimus; quid non properamus et currimus ut patriam nostram uidere et parentes salutare possimus*, 470. 14 *qui . . . per omnes contumelias et poenas superbum populum calcaret et premeret ut contemptus sacerdos de superbo populo ultione diuina uindicaretur.* In the third of these examples the chiastic *patr. par. par. patr.* is to be noticed; in the fourth the recurrence of *c. et p.* in the first, and the repeated words in the middle of both clauses. A more complicated example is 310. 22 *quod interim morimur, ad inmortalitatem morte transgredimur, nec potest uita aeterna succedere nisi hinc contigerit exire. non est exitus iste sed transitus et temporali itinere decurso ad aeterna transgressus.* Here, beside the repetition of *aeterna*, three verbs with their cognates and two prefixes are pressed into the service. Another elaborate instance is 409. 16 ff. *nam cum in illa prima transgressione praecepti firmitas corporis cum inmortalitate discesserit et cum morte infirmitas uenerit, nec possit firmitas recipi nisi cum recepta et inmortalitas fuerit, oportet in hac fragilitate adque infirmitate corporea luctari semper et congredi, quae luctatio et congressio* sq. The stiff monotony of these two passages is not due to carelessness; they are from the most rhetorical of Cyprian's later writings, the *De Bono Patientiae*, and the words were no doubt deliberately chosen and arranged. Similar passages are excessively numerous throughout Cyprian's writings; among the best are those which begin 261. 17, 361. 9, 393. 9, 501. 5, 647. 4, 693. 4. In some instances the language is forced for the sake of symmetry; e.g. 381. 18, where at the end of a long parataxis we read *et dum times ne pro te patrimonium perdas, ipse pro patrimonio pereas*, 493. 16 *hunc igitur agonem per prophetas ante praedictum, per Dominum commissum, per apostolos gestum* sq., 576. 9 *per tales talia perferuntur*. In all these and in many more cases prepositions are used unnaturally for this rhetorical purpose. No stronger instance of Cyprian's attachment to this figure can be found than his consenting to use the unliterary word *deificus* (see ch. ii. § 1) in parataxis with *Deus*; 618. 22 *nec remanere in ecclesia Dei possunt qui deificam et ecclesiasticam disciplinam* sq., and elsewhere. He avoids it in every other context. It remains to mention such prolonged instances as 582. 19 *iacuit inter poenas poenis suis fortior, inclusus includentibus maior, iacens stantibus celsior, uincientibus firmior uinctus, sublimior iudicantibus iudicatus*, and 695. 18 *ut pascendo gregi pastor et gubernandae naui gubernator et plebi regendae rector redderetur* sq. These also are not uncommon in Cyprian.

§ 17. No figure is more common than anaphora in Cyprian; it is constantly used both in prolonging a period and in beginning successive sentences; 319. 5 *insinuantes et docentes hoc esse baptisma in gratia maius, in potestate sublimius, in honore pretiosius, baptisma in quo angeli baptizant, baptisma in* quo Deus et Christus eius exultant, baptisma post quod nemo iam peccat, baptisma quod fidei nostrae incrementa consummat, baptisma quod nos de mundo recedentes statim Deo copulat. in aquae baptismo sq. Not only is *baptisma* carried through the sentence, but Cyprian also, for the sake of symmetry, here uses the vulgar *in* instrumental—*baptisma in quo angeli baptizant*—which is very rare in his writings. This may be compared with his use of *deificus*, mentioned above. Other good instances are 368. 9 ff. *credite illi qui omnino non fallit. credite illi qui haec omnia futura praedixit. credite illi qui credentibus praemium uitae aeternae dabit. credite illi qui incredulis aeterna supplicia gehennae ardoribus inrogabit,* and 731. 6 ff. *dixisti sane scrupulum tibi esse tollendum de animo, in quem incidisti. incidisti, sed tua credulitate inreligiosa. incidisti, sed tua mente et uoluntate sacrilega, dum incesta, dum inpia, dum nefanda contra fratrem, contra sacerdotem facile audis libenter et credis.* In *De Hab. Virg.* §§ 8–11 begin with *locupletem te dicis et diuitem*; in *Mort.* 14 (306. 2 ff.) five short sentences begin with *mori timeat*; in *Ep.* 74. § 8 (805. 16 ff.) are five questions beginning *dat honorem Deo qui,* followed by *si sic honor Deo datur*; in *Ep.* 55. 20 (638. 16 ff.) an eightfold example. Other instances, more or less elaborate and regular, are countless; 359. 18, 672. 5, 595. 9, 829. 18, &c.[1]. In some cases the aim is obviously alliteration, as in 202. 7 *uince uestem quae uirgo es, uince aurum.*

The examples of the same word repeated at the beginning and end of a clause are few; 479. 20 *salutat uos diaconus et qui mecum sunt salutant,* 596. 7 *pacem pollicetur ne perueniri possit ad pacem. salutem promittit ne qui deliquit ueniat ad salutem,* and probably others; cf. 365. 12 *Dei hominem et cultorem Dei,* 414. 19, &c. This is more common with cognate words, as 686. 18 *delictis plus quam quod oportet remittendis paene ipse delinquo,* and with rhyming words[2].

---

[1] Cf. Seneca, *N. Q.* 3 prolog. *quid est praecipuum?* six times repeated.

[2] For this figure cf. Volkmann's *Rhetorik der Gr. u. Römer* 471, and Apuleius, *Met.* 4. 32, 11. 5 (76. 13, 208. 7 Eyss.), though neither is an exact parallel.

230 The Style and Language of St. Cyprian.

§ 18. Asyndeton, not to any noteworthy extent of words, but of clauses, is very characteristic of the style of Cyprian. Especially it is his custom to end long periods with a string of asyndeta; e.g. 5. 18 *tenacibus semper inlecebris necesse est, ut solebat, uinolentia iuuitet, inflet superbia, iracundia inflammet, rapacitas inquietet, crudelitas stimulet, ambitio delectet, libido praecipitet.* In this instance Cyprian was no doubt as much interested in the rhyme as in the asyndeton; but he was so well satisfied with the latter that he has repeated the combination in no less than four other treatises, though less completely and with much variation: 225. 9, 299. 17, 423. 6; cf. 357. 27, which, however, is not asyndetic. Other good examples are 411. 26, 596. 4, 617. 18, 655. 18, 806. 1.

A period formed of two asyndetic clauses of some length, often antithetical, is common, as also an unconnected clause at the end of a period; cf. 412. 7 *docet delinquentibus cito ignoscere, si ipse delinquas diu et multum rogare*, 231. 10, 425. 19, 746. 7, 765. 11, 793. 10. Long asyndetic passages, with anaphora and alliteration, are frequent; *Mort.* § 26 and *Z. L.* §§ 7, 8 are good examples.

Though Cyprian's use of copulative conjunctions is variable and eccentric[1], he does not seem to have used polysyndeton as a rhetorical figure.

§ 19. Amplification by means of synonymous nouns coordinated is common in Cyprian. The simplest form, of two substantives without epithet, is not the most usual. *Preces et orationes*, words without any distinction of meaning in this writer, occurs at least eight times (see p. 269 for this and other pleonasms concerning prayer); *scopulos et saxa* 474. 5[2], *conflictationes et pressurae* 404. 29, *apostatae et desertores uel aduersarii et hostes* 647. 16, *uictimae et hostiae* 195. 21, 652. 24,

---

[1] Cf. the passages beginning 412. 17, 527. 22, 587. 14, 668. 2.

[2] This is a favourite pleonasm of Seneca, *Ben.* 4. 22. 3, *Dial.* 2. 1. 2 *saxa et rupes*, *N. Q.* 2. 6. 5 *scopulos rupesque*, *N. Q.* 3. 12. 2 *saxa cautesque*, *N. Q.* 4. 2. 5 *scopuli cautium*. Apuleius, *Met.* 5. 27 (94. 26 Eyss.) *saxa cautium*, *Met.* 6. 31 (116. 27) *saxum scruposum*. Lucan, 2. 619 *scopulosae rupis*, 5. 675 *scruposis saxis*, Ambr. *Ep.* 6. 13 *scrupea rupes*. Cyprian has *scopulosa saxa* 301. 23.

The Style of St. Cyprian. 231

mora et tarditas 497. 4; cf. 240. 5, 694. 22, and many more. *Aduersarius et Inimicus, episcopi et sacerdotes*, and others, which are practically fixed theological terms, will be found in the next chapter. It may be noted that in 383. 9 ff. there are to be found within eight lines *ineptis et stultis, metu et sollicitudine, secreta et abdita, alta et profunda, captiuus et seruus, catenis et uinculis*; cf. also 309. 24 ff.

It is not very often that one of these coordinated substantives defines the other, as in 310. 18 *uerbis et promissis*, 525. 11 *obsequiis et operibus*, 597. 12 *ex eorum sermone adque adseueratione*, 600. 2 *sinum adque conplexum*; cf. the context. A singular abstract with a plural concrete is more usual; *ui et lapidibus* 408. 22, *in latebris adque in solitudine*, . . . *in febribus et in languore* 654. 2 f.; so 659. 23, 666. 1, 679. 4, 688. 11, &c.

Adjectives are often similarly joined; 363. 18 *clarum adque manifestum*, 257. 12 *abdita et secreta*, 618. 14 *similia et paria*, 268. 26, 780. 9, &c. This is more usual than two identical adjectives attached to a substantive; *parua et modica delicta* 682. 3, and again 786. 21, *sub regali ac tyrannica seruitute* 337. 21, *eiusmodi et tales serui* 567. 21; cf. Novatian in *Ep.* 30 (555. 23) *episcopi uicini et adpropinquantes*.

It is more usual for Cyprian to double both epithet and substantive; *fama mendax et falsus rumor* 601. 7, *dissimulatio nulla, nulla cunctatio* 358. 23; for this use of *dissimulatio* see p. 301, *pares ambo et uterque consimiles* 584. 8, *proxima mors et uicina arcessitio* 298. 25, *mandata diuina ac praecepta caelestia* 338. 12, 378. 21, and often; cf. 356. 18, 419. 11, 422. 25, 580. 20, 798. 14, &c.

Double adverbs are also common; 290. 8 *sollicite et caute*, 649. 12 *incaute et temere*, 309. 24 *merito ac iure*, 648. 1 *uberius ac plenius*, &c.; cf. 675. 12 *ultro et crimine suo perire*. But as a rule they are employed for alliteration rather than simply to fill out the sentence.

When synonymous and even not synonymous nouns are preceded by a preposition, this preposition is often repeated for the sake of symmetry; 505. 23 *in arto et in angusto*

232 The Style and Language of St. Cyprian.

itinere, 593. 4 *a uultibus adque ab oculis uestris*, ib. 11 *per minas et per insidias perfidorum*, 731. 20 *in carcere et in catenis*. In the two last alliteration is partly the motive. Other instances of such repeated prepositions are 404. 12, 421. 4, 606. 10, 641. 22, 654. 2, 3, 6.

When synonymous verbs and participles are coordinated, it is more usually with a view to alliteration than to simple amplification. For such forms as *addimus et adiungimus, recreati et renati*, &c. see § 15. Cyprian's otiose manner of citing Scripture is mentioned in the next chapter, § 6. In addition to the examples cited there, good instances will be found in *Ep.* 74. §§ 3, 11 and *Laps.* 15. Beside such cases there are many others, e.g. *uereris et metuis* 380. 8, *festinat et properat* 414. 27, *adgnoscant adque intellegant* 599. 4, *quam* (sc. *persecutionem*) *iste uoto quodam euadendae et lucrandae*[1] *damnationis excipiens haec omnia commisit et miscuit, ut qui eici de ecclesia et excludi habebat* sq. 619. 12, *Goliath interfecto et ope ac dignatione diuina tanto hoste deleto* 422. 12.

There are some instances of double synonymous phrases; 196. 12 *fugiant castae uirgines et pudicae incestarum cultus, habitus inpudicarum, lupanarum*[2] *insignia, ornamenta meretricum*; cf. 363. 11 *ruinis rerum, iacturis opum, dispendio militum, deminutione castrorum*[3].

Though Cyprian's usual amplification may be expressed by the formula AB + AB, in some cases he varies it by doubling the qualifying synonym in the second half, thus using the form AB + AAB; e.g. 388. 21 *bis delinquis et geminum ac duplex crimen admittis*, 601. 1 *neque enim facile promenda sunt et incaute ac temere publicanda quae* sq.[4]; cf. 365. 18 *exul-*

---

[1] For *lucrari = effugere* see p. 308.

[2] Cf. 699. 25 *lenonum et lupanarum insignia*; see Haussleiter in Wölfflin's *Archiv*, 8. 145, Wölfflin, ib. p. 8, on *Spect.* 5 (App. 8. 5), and Georges' *Lexicon, s.v.* In all these cases *lupana = meretrix*.

[3] I. e. *exercituum*, as in 693. 11 and elsewhere in Cyprian.

[4] There are other instances to which the references are unfortunately lost; quite sufficient in all to prove that this form is no accident, but a deliberate rhetorical device. I have not noticed it in Apuleius.

The Style of St. Cyprian. 233

tant semper in Domino et laetantur et gaudent in Deo suo, 669. 9, &c.

Clauses identical in meaning are not uncommon; e. g. 249. 17 *nemo se fallat, nemo decipiat*, 195. 7 *diuitem te sentiant pauperes, locupletem te sentiant indigentes*, 581. 7 *quoniam semper gaudium properat nec potest moras ferre laetitia*, 426. 2 ff., a triple instance, 247. 2, 363. 12, &c. So Novatian in *Ep.* 30 (553. 20) *non sit minor medicina quam uulnus est, non sint minora remedia quam funera*[1], and probably the same writer in *Ep.* 36 (572. 12).

It was naturally more difficult to find three synonyms than to find two, and therefore cases are less common in Cyprian, though by no means rare; e. g. 198. 7 *opus Dei et factura eius et plastica*, 305. 6 *infirmitas et inbecillitas et uastitas*, 284. 22 *pacificos et concordes adque unanimes*, 400. 11 *quisque lenis patiens et mitis est*, 720. 15 *adultos et prouectos et maiores natu*, 310. 1 *si simulata, si ficta, si fucata uidentur esse quae dicimus*, ib. 4 *inprobat denique apostolus Paulus et obiurgat et culpat*, 377. 16 *reuelat angelus et manifestat et firmat*, 618. 3 *hostis quietis, tranquillitatis aduersarius, pacis inimicus*, 318. 3 *circumuenit nescium, fallit incautum, decipit inperitum*; this last is preceded by three *si* clauses.

The subordination of synonymous substantives is also very common; 217. 23, 220. 17 *concordia pacis*, 285. 11 *concordiae pax*, 222. 1 *zeli discordia*, 198. 20, 226. 11 *temeritatis audacia*, 284. 14 *uigor censurae*, 744. 16 *censura uigoris*, 301. 8 *morbi ualetudo*, 5. 10, 15. 26 *senium uetustatis*, 618. 23 *actus conuersatio*, 200. 13 *sermonum conloquia* (cf. *sermo conloquii* in *Ep.* 75, 826. 8), 721. 17 *lapsus ruinae*, 201. 10 *amictus uestis*, 7. 14, 806. 11 *uenenorum uirus*, 502. 17, 503. 20, 632. 19 *exitus mortis*, 490. 11 *certaminis proelium*, 202. 11, 214. 12, 228. 19, 231. 6, 318. 15, 500. 15, 617. 1, 775. 10, &c. So

---

[1] Novatian had certainly learned rhetoric in the same school with Cyprian and Apuleius. His attempts at effect in language are the same as theirs. His characteristic difference from both is the parade of logical method, in syllogism, &c. The three writers are of course widely different in vocabulary.

234 The Style and Language of St. Cyprian.

with gerunds; 194. 11 *concupiscendi libido*, 602. 14 *ambigendi scrupulus*, 479. 11 *introeundi aditus*. Instances where the dependent substantive is of narrower application than the other are frequent, e.g. *hospitium carceris* 494. 2, 577. 22, *carcerum claustra* 828. 8, *custodia carceris* 582. 15, *obsequium operationis* 503. 18 (cf. 525. 11), *subsidium cibi* 283. 10, *quantitas numeri* 338. 7, *uoluntatis imperium* 308. 16, *conuiciorum probra, contumeliarum ludibria* 402. 9, 10. Two synonymous nouns combined with a synonymous genitive occur 373. 18 *fragilitatis humanae infirmitas atque inbecillitas*.

A synonymous substantive and adjective also stand often together; 15. 5 *inmortalitas aeterna*, 301. 23 *scopulosa saxa*, 355. 26 *morbida ualetudo*, 421. 11 *maliuolus liuor*, 422. 11 *mitis lenitas*, 578. 13 *multiplex numerositas*, 583. 14 *generosa nobilitas*, 644. 11 *caenosa uorago* (cf. in *Ep.* 75 *uorago et caenum* 824. 21), 702. 1 *ultronea uoluntate* = *ultro*, 783. 6 *adumbrata simulatio*, 364. 20 *aeuum temporale*, 35. 10, 224. 2 *conpendium breuians*, 7. 17 *increpantes minae*, 287. 6 *collecta breuitas*; cf. 272. 8[1]. I have only noticed one instance of a double synonymous adjective with a synonymous substantive, 313. 4 *turbida et procellosa tempestas* (cf. 501. 21, 618. 2).

Examples of a synonym or synonyms under a government different from that of the adjective are also frequent, e.g. 189. 21 *cauti ad sollicitudinem*, 214. 6 *exuudantis copiae largitas*, 230. 20 *aliqua fallentis astutiae calliditate decepti*, 250. 3 *praepropera festinatione temerarius* (and similarly 528. 9), 424. 25 *remedium curae medentis*, 578. 11 *inmota et inconcussa fide stabiles*, 624. 22 *aestuantis animi sollicitudo suspensa*, 689. 3 *inbecillitate humanae mediocritatis inualidus*, 617. 20 *auaritiae inexplebilis rapacitate furibundus, adrogantia et stupore superbi tumoris inflatus*, 192. 12, 357. 28, 422. 11, 478. 12, 807. 17, &c.

Otiose pronouns are not uncommon. It is, of course, possible that many of these are not inserted for purposes of rhetoric, but simply through carelessness. Yet the large number of similar cases in Apuleius and Arnobius makes it

---

[1] Similarly in 501. 17 *exiguam stantium paucitatem* should probably be read.

The Style of St. Cyprian. 235

certain that this was a rhetorical device in Cyprian also. A curious coordination occurs twice; 668. 14 *conuicia eorum quibus se et uitam suam cottidie lacerant*, 718. 13 *nobis enim adque oculis nostris . . . accipere qui nati sunt incrementum uidentur*; cf. in the Roman *Ep.* 36 (572. 16) *nos adque animum nostrum*. The apposition *nos, ego et Liberalis* occurs 606. 9. The repetition of antecedent after relative is rare; 498. 10 *iuuene qui iuuenis*, 752. 21 *agni qui agnus*, and 720. 5; cf. 773. 1 *ut quia ouis iam fuerat hanc ouem . . . pastor recipiat.*

But most of the examples in Cyprian are of the repetition of a personal or demonstrative pronoun under the same or a different construction, in either case without helping the sense[1]. So 607. 7 *nos enim singulis nauigantibus . . . nos scimus hortatos esse ut* sq., 623. 6 *ut se putet . . . palam iam ferre se posse* (the true reading), 587. 17 *ut etiam nunc ego . . . omnes opto me nosse* = 'I wish to know all;' cf. 276. 20 *et ideo Christiani qui in oratione appellare patrem Deum coepimus nos et ut regnum Dei nobis ueniat oramus.* A superfluous demonstrative pronoun appears after a substantive or a relative, e.g. 593. 23 (*presbyteri*) *qui ad duorum presbyterorum ueterem nequitiam respondentes, sicut illi Susannam pudicam corrumpere et uiolare conati sunt, sic et hi adulterinis doctrinis ecclesiae pudicitiam corrumpere . . . conantur*, 615. 10 *in confessoribus . . . nemo non socium se et participem eorum gloriae conputat*, 784. 16 *quod autem quidam dicunt eis qui in Samaria baptizati fuerant . . . tantum super eos manum inpositam esse*; cf. ib. 24, 606. 12, 638. 6, &c. Possessives are often used needlessly; 7. 4 *si iustitiae uiam teneas inlapsa firmitate uestigii tui*, 340. 19 *mater . . . tam grande martyrium Deo praebens uirtute oculorum suorum quam praebuerant filii eius tormentis et passione membrorum*; for *suus* a large collection, which can be at least doubled, is given by Hartel *s.v.* The superfluous *eius* has a similar use; to Hartel's list *s.v. is* may be added, 423. 18,

---

[1] Cf. Apul. *Met.* 5. 25 (93. 20 Eyss.) *nec te rursus praecipitio uel ullo mortis accersito te genere perimas*; Gell. 2. 3. 1 *H litteram . . . inserebant eam ueteres* sq.; Arnobius 7. 30 (264. 17 Reiff.), &c., with Hildebrand's note, p. 499.

503. 14, 595. 25, 670. 8, and many more. *Deus et Christus eius*, if the *eius* be superfluous, is mentioned in the next chapter, § 4.

Such uses as 582. 26 *et si aliquis Thomae similis extiterit qui minus auribus credat, nec oculorum fides deest ut quis quod audit et uideat*, and 547. 12 *ne quid conscientiam uestram lateret quid mihi scriptum sit, quidque ego rescripserim* are not uncommon; *quis* is a pronoun which Cyprian used often and sometimes strangely[1]: *quid deinde illud, quale est ut* or *quod* sq., *quid deinde illud, quam* sq., and similar phrases are used several times in rhetorical questions; 9. 6, 307. 3. 359. 16, 507. 20, 792. 12, and elsewhere.

Otiose pronouns in apposition are rare in Cyprian and not remarkable, e. g. *hic idem* 570. 4, 584. 20, *is ipse* 359. 16, 583. 23, and, as a substitute for *quisquis*, *talis . . . quisque* 225. 25; cf. *quod totum hoc* in *Ep.* 75 (811. 27)[2].

A verb synonymous with its subject or a participle with the noun in agreement, occurs several times; 213. 1, 4 *originem ab uno incipientem . . . exordium ab unitate proficiscitur*, 542. 12 *denique huius seditionis origo iam coepit*, 398. 25, &c.; synonymous with an adjective 490. 4 *exulto laetus et gratulor*[3], 488. 23 *cum opinio dubia nutaret*, 430. 17 *oratio ingis omnino non cesset*, &c.; with the adjective as object 360. 12 *multiplicas*

---

[1] But these may be merely careless language, as is that of Caldonius, 537 13 *ne quid uidear temere aliquid praesumere.*

[2] To syntax rather than to style belongs the use of *plusquam quod* for *plusquam*, e.g. 687. 15 *aut plus existimemus ad inpugnandum posse humana conamina quam quod ad protegendum praeualeat diuina tutela*, cf. 321. 10, 526. 14, 686. 19, and elsewhere; but in 623. 10 the *quod* is omitted. *Illud* or *hoc* introducing an *ut, quod* or acc. inf. clause is frequent, 305. 14, 547. 15, 713. 20, 756. 6, 765. 5, 799. 14. Through the weakening of *ut* as a final particle—its normal use in Cyprian is consecutive or explanatory—*ad hoc* or *propter hoc* are used, the former especially, to give the final sense to *ut* or *ne*. To Hartel's list of the former may be added 14. 8, 15. 8, 102. 23 and very many more; *propter hoc ut* 839. 12, *propter hoc . . . ne* 653. 9, *propter hoc quod* 756. 9. Similarly, to strengthen *quod, hoc ipso, ex hoc ipso*, &c. are often used, e.g. 321. 1, 406. 14, 720. 22, &c., cf. *hoc ipso si* 195. 15, *hoc ipso quo* 387. 14, 512. 4, *hoc ipso quia* 693. 4.

[3] *Gratulari = gaudere* is common in Cyprian; cf. 545. 6 *laetatus satis et plurimum gratulatus quod* sq.; see p. 308.

The Style of St. Cyprian. 237

numerosa supplicia. A synonymous adverb and verb are also common: 569. 2 *pertinaciter persistere*, 707. 17 *rursus iterare*, 540. 3 *nec delicto priori adiciant adhuc aliud delictum* (cf. 249. 22, 254. 3, 792. 17), 5. 6 *denuo renasci*, 640. 10 *denuo redire*, 591. 11 *denuo renouare*, 391. 8 *ante praedicere*, which is very common. Indeed verbs formed with *prae* are usually preceded by *ante*, as *ante praeuenire* 347. 14, *ante praemittere* 720. 1, *ante praemonere* 768. 22, *ante praestruere* 209. 11, *ante praemonstrare* 704. 12. Both *denuo* and *ante* occur together in 706. 13 *denuo praecanitur et ante praedicitur*, unless, as is very probable, *item denuo* go together. Instances of a synonymous verb and noun connected by a preposition are not frequent; 15. 26 *non haec unquam procumbet in lapsum senio uetustatis*, 188. 22 *per omnia seruitutis obsequia Redemptoris imperio pareamus*, 431. 13 *ut diuina et spiritalis seges in copiam fecundae messis exuberet*, 785. 17 *arbores frugiferas intra muros suos intus inclusit*, 243. 17, 362. 20, &c. *Nisi cum Trofimo comitante uenissent*, 632. 3, may be classed with these, and 577. 8 *reuertentis anni uolubilem circulum*. A synonymous ablative is more common, usually in elaborate phrases containing other forms of amplification; 424. 5 *quantoque ille cui inuidetur successu meliore profecerit tanto inuidus in maius incendium liuoris ignibus inardescit*, 293. 20 *quando mundi lege decurrens uicibus alternis nox reuoluta succedit*, 643. 23 *quando ... uasa lignea diuini ardoris incendio concrementur*, 670. 7 *cum tormentis cruciabundus flammae cremantis ardoribus aduratur*, 576. 16 *cum in secessu priuatis precibus oramus*, and similarly 275. 18, 501. 9, 567. 2, &c., 724. 7 *cenis adque epulis etiam nunc inhiant quarum crapulam super superstitem in dies cruditate ructabant*, and many more. Cf. the periphrastic *amor quo diligis* 4. 5, *cari quos diligimus* 300. 25.

Temporal and local adverbs are often combined, others rarely. *Diu multumque differtur* 400. 7, 412. 8, 623. 14, *festinato statim* 676. 3, *seorsum foris* 672. 9; cf. *primo et inter initia* 625. 13. *Iamiamque* seems only to occur once, 833. 7; *tandem iam* 726. 10. *Quando adhuc et*, strictly temporal, is read, 477. 1[1]. An adverb with a synonymous prepositional expression is very common, though the adverbs so employed are few; *hic in ecclesia* 584. 17, *illic in carcere* 576. 10, *illic apud clericos* 479. 3, *illinc a uobis* 618. 4, *inde ad nos* 617. 18, *istic in mundo* 301. 14, *istic apud fratres* 678. 17, *istinc de saeculo* 310. 13, *intus in ecclesia* 647. 16, *foris extra ecclesiam* 214. 25, are instances of the usual types. *Statim* is often similarly used; *in primo statim natiuitatis exordio* 243. 11, *a primo statim persecutionis die* 679. 21, 210. 3, 272. 20, 337. 2, 401. 10, 405. 18, 482. 1, 721. 9, &c.; so also *adhuc* 354. 3, 797. 21. An adverb synonymous with an adjective occurs 272. 8 *breuiter collecta* (cf. *collecta breuitas* 287. 6), 808. 10 *quo minus aqua continua perseueranter ac iugiter flueret*, 519. 15 *quando ipsa ante mater nostra pacem . . . prior sumpserit*; cf. 421. 11 *non prius alterum deiciens . . . quam ipse zelo ante deiectus*, and 695. 6. Two very Apuleian expressions are 541. 3 *libellos gregatim multis dare* and 598. 21, cited above, p. 201. There remain the otiose uses of *magis*[2] and *adhuc*. *Magis ac magis* is used at least twelve times, 225. 8, &c., *magis* followed by a comparative thrice; 397. 10 *quid magis sit uel utilius ad uitam uel maius ad gloriam quam* sq.[3], 420. 19, 583. 17. *Magis* is followed by an otiose *plus* 513. 12. *Adhuc* is used like *magis* to strengthen a comparative; to Hartel's instances add 356. 9, 357. 21, 694. 1; *adhuc magis* together 404. 8, *ultra adhuc* 287. 12 and 667. 2, *adhuc insuper*[4] 359.

---

[1] *Et tunc quidem gladio occidebantur, quando adhuc et circumcisio carnalis manebat.* Hartel's statement, *s. v. quando*, that the word is used *perraro* with the indicative is an overstatement. The instances, both temporal and logical, are fairly numerous.

[2] This adverb, which gives Cyprian great difficulty, has many irregular uses, not given in Hartel's *Index*, which belong rather to syntax than to style. *Magis tam*, of which he gives two instances, also occurs 549. 17, but is confined to the Roman letters.

[3] This is not carelessness, but no doubt a superfluous word introduced for parallelism with the *maius* that follows. It is at the opening of *De Bono Pat.*, and Cyprian always bestows his best rhetoric upon the beginning and end of his writings.

[4] *Adhuc insuper* is confined to a short period of Cyprian's writings. It occurs four times in *Ep.* 59, once in 67, once in 73, twice in *Ad Dem.*, once in

22, 24, 681. 2, &c., *adhuc insuper et* 404. 19, *post ista adhuc insuper* 683. 8, *et post ista adhuc insuper et* 685. 13 (cf. *et post ista adhuc* 403. 1), *immo adhuc insuper* 779. 16. *Adhuc usque* 495. 18, 679. 13 appears to be first used by Tertullian; *quoad usque* 301. 14 had been already used in the O. L. Bible.

Copulative conjunctions are constantly multiplied; *et . . . quoque* 598. 5, *nec . . . quoque* 427. 22, *etiam . . . et* 677. 22, *adhuc quoque* 750. 13, *sed et* constantly (see Hartel's *Index*), *sed nec, sed neque* 319. 21, 390. 9, 517, 11, 631. 14, 805. 1, &c., *nec non et* 238. 14, 318. 23, 339. 19, &c., *nec non . . . quoque* 409. 14; cf. *nec non etiam . . . quoque* of Novatian, 551. 12. *Pariter et* is of constant occurrence, e. g. 600. 11, 21, almost always connecting long words; *simul et* is rare; to Hartel's list should perhaps be added 510. 3; *similiter et* only 399. 8. *Denuo quoque* occurs 190. 8, *item denuo* often, 374. 6, 751. 2, &c. *Porro autem* is common in Cyprian's latest writings, 374. 21, 419. 7, and in the *Epp.* on the Baptismal controversy. The only earlier instance is in *Ep.* 58, 659. 8. *Scilicet certe* is read once, in a badly written passage, 339. 8. The list of otiose conjunctions might be made much longer.

Prepositions are used otiosely with *uicarius* and *solus*; *pro me . . . uicarias litteras* 480. 13, and similarly 587. 13, 656. 14, 697. 20, *me solum sine uobis* 593. 6 and so 294. 12; cf. 594. 23 *sibi soli*.

It remains to notice certain cases of *contingere, debere, esse, posse* used simply to expand the sentence; 432. 12 *peruenire . . . ut eum uidere contingat* = *uideamus,* 547. 5 *quorum tempora inlustrauit tanta felicitas ut aetate nostra uidere contingeret probatos seruos Dei* sq., 509. 13 *quamquam causa conpelleret ut ipse ad uos properare et uenire deberem,* and similarly 827. 21 [1];

B. Pat.; once also in *Ep.* 75 (826. 8). The combination is not noticed by Georges under either word.

[1] Yet this *debere* may be purely auxiliary; cf. Cod. Lugd. Gen. 29. 21 *ut introire deberem* = ὅπως εἰσέλθω, cited by Thielmann in Wolfflin's *Archiv,* 2. 65, and 487. 6 in the Roman *Ep.* 8. *Coepisse* and *incipere* are certainly used by Cyprian as strict auxiliaries.

510. 22 *si qui sunt qui ... indigeant*, 502. 11 *utinam loci conditio permitteret ut ipse nunc praesens esse possem*, 404. 17, 505. 12, &c.; cf. 602. 18, cited on p. 222. *Videri*, again, is used superfluously in a number of passages where there is certainly no idea of seeming, as 309. 27 *spei nostrae et fidei praevaricatores sumus, si simulata, si ficta, si fucata uidentur esse quae dicimus*, where *uidentur esse* must be for *sunt*; cf. 223. 15, 227. 10, 714. 8, 761. 10, 809. 12, &c.[1]

§ 20. Hitherto examples of amplification have been chosen which were not cases of *figura etymologica*, or other rhetorical devices. Of *figura etymologica* in the strict sense[2] there are not many instances in Cyprian. Taking them in Landgraf's order, the following is perhaps a complete list; 259. 15 *induere indumenta*, 432. 11 *curricula decurrere*, 578. 21 *uita uiuitur*, 512. 4 *superantem superare*, 621. 17 and 725. 9 *tenere tenorem*, 710. 14 *polo poculo*[3]; 425. 21 *inluminati Christi lumine*, 501. 7 *oratione communi ... orantes*, 672. 8 *discidio scindere* (cf. 231. 9), 768. 14 *unctione unctus*; 728. 14 *episcopum episcopi et iudicem iudicis*; 3. 4 *tempestiuum tempus*, 238. 2 and 723. 15 *sacrificia sacrilega*, 399. 5 *sacra sacrilega*; 465. 4 and 581. 5 *praesens adesse*; 408. 19 and constantly *omnis omnino*; 473. 2 *continenter tenere*. Besides these there only remains *magis ac magis*, already mentioned; *magis magisque* is never used by Cyprian.

§ 21. Sufficient evidence has been given to show that Cyprian's style is that of a man so thoroughly trained in a rhetorical school that he never, even in his most hasty writing, fails to show his education. It is a style which is essentially

---

[1] Some instances are purely passive, as 622. 15 *etsi uidentur in ecclesia esse zizania*, which states that they are, not that they seem to be, present, 673. 19 *cum talis ... inpugnari uidetur, apparet quis inpugnet*. There is a strange passive use of *uideri* in *De Rebapt.* 7 (A 78. 9).

[2] As defined by G. Landgraf in *Acta Seminarii Philologici Erlangensis*, vol. ii. pp. 1-69, 'conpositio duorum congenerum uocabulorum quae item grammaticae legibus artissime inter se conexa unam eamque amplificatam atque disertissimam notionem efficiant.'

[3] The frequent *oblationem offerre*, since it is a fixed part of the Christian vocabulary, cannot be regarded as an instance of *accusatiuus etymologicus*.

one with that of Apuleius, and had no doubt been learnt by both on African soil. But how far it was peculiar to Africa is a more doubtful point. In its literary aspect it is closely akin to that of Ammianus and the Panegyrists; in its grammatical to that of Vitruvius [1]. Though it is certain that provincial peculiarities existed, and certain also that many of them have been detected, yet the unconscious degeneration of grammar and the conscious efforts after rotundity of expression were common to the whole empire. A constant emigration seems to have been going on from southern Italy to Carthage, as now to Buenos Ayres, and the connexion between Rome and Africa could not have been closer than it was. Africans of Roman descent no doubt did their best to retain, and the educated natives to assume, the characteristics in language and otherwise of Italians. It is therefore dangerous to regard as peculiarities of African writers what may only appear to be such, because comparatively little has survived of the literature of other provinces in the third century. What would have been the strongest possible evidence, could it have been sustained, a Semitic element in African Latin, has been abandoned by the author of the theory [2]. There are of course local elements in the style of Cyprian as of other writers, and the present tendency of inquirers is certainly not to underestimate them; but his style is undoubtedly that of an educated, though careless, Latin writer, trained in and satisfied with the fashions of his day. There is no sign that he had any training but the rhetorical. Legal terms occasionally occur; but every Roman knew something of law, and nothing indicates that Cyprian had a professional knowledge. Of philosophy, in spite of his acquaintance with Seneca, he shows no sign. That formal logic, of which Novatian makes so pedantic a display, and in which his

[1] As set out in J. Praun's *Bemerkungen zur Syntax des Vitruv*, Bamberg, 1885.
[2] K. Sittl, *Lokale Verschiedenheiten*, p. 92 ff. He surrenders it, with some reservations, in the *Jahresbericht*, 1892, p. 246. Yet is not *unctus Dei* for *a Deo* 768. 14 a Hebraism?

philosophy, derided by Cyprian, appears to have consisted [1], is never employed. His full command of all the technical devices of the rhetorician, chastened only to some extent by the seriousness of his thought, his amplitude of expression and the smoothness with which his periods move—it would be possible to collect from the few pages of Cornelius almost as many abrupt transitions as from all Cyprian's writings,— the copiousness and originality of his vocabulary, all display him as one who exercised the thoughts and the culture of the old world upon the problems of the new. It is recognized now that the older scholars were wrong in classing together all the Christian authors as writers of ecclesiastical Latin. No such Latin existed till the monasteries were established, and the great Fathers had written. And there is no author to whose style the term can be less appropriately applied than Cyprian.

[1] Fronto also (*De Eloquentia*, p. 146, Naber) appears to regard formal logic as of the essence of philosophy, and ridicules it accordingly. Cf. Ps.-Apul. *De Dogm. Plat.* iii. p 272 Oud. (ed. Goldbacher in *Wiener Studien*, 1885, p. 267. 10), and Apul. *Flor.* 1. 7

CHAPTER II.

LANGUAGE.

§ 1. *Deus*, &c. § 2. Divine action, creation, miracles, law. § 3. Divine favour and disfavour. § 4. Christ and His work. § 5. The Holy Spirit, prophecy, visions. § 6. Scripture. § 7. Types. § 8. *Christianus, fidelis*, &c. § 9. *Ecclesia*, &c. § 10. Laity. § 11. Bishop. § 12. Other Orders and Ordination. § 13. Councils. § 14. Proselytes and catechumens. § 15. Baptism and accompanying Rites. § 16. The Eucharist. § 17. Prayer. § 18. The place of worhsip. § 19. Preaching. § 20. Manner of address, *frater*, &c. § 21. Payment of the clergy. § 22. Christian virtues. § 23. Alms. § 24. Christian conduct and progress. § 25. Sin and Penitence. § 26. Freewill and conscience. § 27. Death and Heaven. § 28. The devil and hell. § 29. World and Heathen. § 30. Persecution, Confession, Martyrdom and Lapse. § 31. Heresy. § 32. Greek words. § 33. New and rare substantives. § 34. Adjectives. § 35. Pronouns. § 36. Verbs. § 37. Adverbs and Conjunctions. § 38. Prepositions, &c.

IN this chapter the attempt is made to give a full account of the theological and ecclesiastical terms used by Cyprian. The subject is that of language, not of doctrine or history, and though the latter cannot be avoided, and indeed it is hoped that this paper may be of use for their study, they have not been introduced except in illustration of the words employed. Illustration from other writers has been avoided, and the history of words before and after Cyprian's day passed over, unless light could in some way be thrown upon Cyprian's motive in using them. Biblical terms also, and especially those of St. Paul, have been omitted, as belonging to the common stock of all Christian writers.

In Cyprian's day the Latin tongue was still adjusting itself to the Faith, and the Christian vocabulary was unsettled. Cyprian was one of those who had most influence in fixing it. A good deal may be learnt, not only from the words

The Style and Language of St. Cyprian.

which he used, but from those which he avoided or attempted to displace, of the course of Christian thought as well as of the Latin language. His hostility to Greek terms, for instance, which I have illustrated, must be regarded as an early sign of severance between Eastern and Western Christendom. But the limits of this paper leave room only for the statement of facts, not for the drawing of conclusions. I have concluded with a selection of new and rare words, not of Christian significance. Want of space has compelled me to omit much that is interesting in this respect.

§ 1. *Deus*, with Cyprian's love for abstracts, is paraphrased in many ways, e.g. 519. 16 *quando ... nos diuina protectio reduces ad ecclesiam suam fecerit*; 680. 16 *ne uulneratos diuina clementia in ecclesia sua curet*; *diuina censura* 496. 19, 737. 8, &c.; *diuina maiestas, pietas, benignitas, bonitas, indulgentia, dignatio* 250. 21, 274. 5, 579. 3, &c.

Deitas is not used by Cyprian. It first occurs in *De Aleatt.* 7 (A 100. 9); an evidence, as far as it goes, for the later authorship of that tract. *Diuinitas*, in the only passage where Cyprian uses it (339. 26), perhaps stands for *diuinatio*, though a comparison with 661. 19 renders this doubtful. *Trinitas* occurs 292. 6, 782. 4, 791. 22, after Tertullian; *diuina firmitas* 215. 7 must mean union of Persons.

Though *Dominus*, when it stands alone, is normally for *Christus*, yet *Deus* and *Dominus* are also used interchangeably and in combination; for rhetorical purposes they often occur at the ends of parallel clauses, e.g. 232. 22 *diem Domini et iram Dei*, 757. 3 *dignatione Dei et ordinatione Domini*. In 320. 13 *praeferamus ... Deum et Christum diabolo et antichristo* Cyprian has gained three rhetorical figures at the cost of one false antithesis.

Beside *diuinus* the adjective *deificus* occurs. The word, which seems to belong to vulgar Latin [1], is used rarely and

---

[1] It is used by the illiterate Lucianus in *Ep.* 22 (533. 12), in *De Aleatt.* 11 (A 103. 16), several times in the *De Montibus*, by the translator of *Ep.* 75 (815 4), in *Sent.* 8 (441. 9). Cyprian only uses the word thrice, and each time deliberately, for the sake of parataxis with *Deus*; 429. 15, 618. 22, 742.

only for a special rhetorical purpose instead of the usual *diuinus*, for which *caelestis* is a frequent substitute. *Dominicus*, which is very common, seems to be used indefinitely, e. g. 430. 16 *sit in manibus diuina lectio, in sensibus dominica cogitatio*, where the words are simply used for variety, as with *Deus* and *Dominus* above. as well as in the strict sense, e. g. *dominica confessio* (of Christ) 319. 15. 656. 21, though the latter is more usual. *Dominicus* (sc. *dies*) = Sunday 581. 8; for *dominicum* = *eucharistia* see p. 266; *spiritalis*, in the corresponding sense, is also common [1].

§ 2. Divine action is often expressed by *diuinitus*, 432. 1, 689. 4, &c.; by *prouidenter*, for alliteration, 607. 19; by *desuper* in 356. 7 for the same reason; by *caelitus* in the rhetorical *Ad Donatum*, 6. 5. Similarly *spiritaliter*, e. g. *quod spiritaliter praecipitur = a Spiritu sancto*, 713. 19; cf. *humanitus laedunt persecutiones*, i. e. 'inflicted by men,' 366. 10.

Acts of power such as miracles are *magnalia, mirabilia*, both several times, *magnalia et mirabilia* 674. 9, *mirabilia uirtutum* 401. 8, *uirtutes* 223. 17, and often. *Miraculum* occurs in the sense of *miratio* 581. 3, 583. 23, not in that of miracle. The nearest approach to it is 582. 15 *conluctationis miraculum = conluctatio mirabilis*; cf. 195. 1 *quibus multa magnalia cum miraculo faceret = mirifice* [2].

Cyprian does not often mention the work of creation [3].

---

21. In 429. 15, 742. 21 there is the further reason that to write *diuina disciplina*, as would have been natural, would be contrary to his rules of composition; see p. 223. Tertullian's *deus deificus* (active) in *Apol.* 11 is probably a coinage of his own; the word is carefully avoided by the more classical of the Christian writers; even Lucifer and Lactantius, in spite of their debt to Cyprian, reject it. It certainly in Cyprian has no meaning other than that of *diuinus*; cf. *regifico luxu* Virgil. *Aen.* 6. 605, *castificus* Sen. *Phaedr.* 169.

[1] Beside this use *spiritalis* is constantly used as practically equivalent to *Christianus* or *sincerus*, e. g. 428. 10, 545. 9, 583. 8. *Caelestis* and *spiritalis* are very often combined; 192. 22, 239. 9, 320. 20, 621. 8, &c.

[2] This use of *cum* is very common in Cyprian; 588. 15 *cum pace = pacifice*, 232. 10 *cum fiducia = fidenter*, &c.

[3] Of the numerous passages in which the Vulgate has *Creator, creare, creatura*, there are singularly few in Cyprian. The only one of these words

246 The Style and Language of St. Cyprian.

Creare, I think, does not occur, *creatura* twice, in a concrete sense, 708. 12, 768. 17, *creator* only 792. 4 *negans Deum creatorem Christi*[1]. *Facere* seems to be the usual equivalent for *creare*, with *factor*, 662. 7, 718. 15; cf. 319. 19[2], and *factura*, in a rhetorical passage, 198. 7. In the *De Hab. Virg.*, adapted from Tertullian, he borrows that writer's *plastica* and *protoplastus* 198. 7, 190. 15; *plasmare* in 804. 18 is an allusion to Sap. 15. 11; *diuinum plasma*, 468. 12, is some evidence that *Ep.* 2 belongs to an earlier date than O. Ritschl's arguments indicate. When Cyprian's style was matured he avoided, as far as possible, the use of Greek words. *Instituere* is used for *creare* 201. 28, *institutio* 468. 10; *institutor* is so used by Tertullian and Lactantius. *Artifex* is used 198. 20, 201. 27, not, I think, *opifex*, though *opus* is found, 198. 7, &c.[3]

The usual words for God's law and appointment are *dispositio* (*Test.* 1. 11 *tit. dispositio et testamentum*), *institutio, ordinatio, traditio*, and *lex*[4]. *Praescriptio* in the legal sense seems the

which they contain is *creatura*, Ecclus. 24. 5, Col. 1. 15 (62. 15, 63. 16). In Dan. 14. 4 (337. 20, 661. 13) and Mal. 2. 10 (114. 16) *condere* takes the place of the Vulgate *creare*. In Eph. 4. 24 κτισθείς is translated by *constitutus* (124. 23) instead of *creatus*, as in the Vulgate. There are no other passages in which *creare* or its cognates might have been expected. In the contemporary *Ad Nov.* 4 (A 56. 13) Gen. 6. 7 reads *perdam hominem quem feci*.

[1] This seems a reference to Heb. 3. 2, where Clarom. reads *creatori suo*, and the Old Latin MSS. generally that or *qui creauit eum*; Vulgate *ei qui fecit illum*. There is another possible reference to Heb. 4. 12 in 271. 21 *inpetrabilis et efficax sermo*. Since Tertullian knew the Epistle it is incredible that Cyprian was ignorant of it, though he would not cite it as Scripture.

[2] *Creare* is not even used, when it might naturally have been expected, of the divine appointment of Bishops, but always *facere, constituere*, &c., though *creare pseudoepiscopum* occurs 642. 22. In fact, through its use by Marcion, the word seems to have gained a heretical connotation, of which this may be a survival. Tertullian very rarely uses it except in reference to the *deus Marcionis* (*Adu. Marc.* constantly, *Carn. Xti* 2, *Res. Carn.* 2, *Prax.* 3, &c.), the true God being *conditor*. *Soter* has similarly suffered through Gnostic use (Tert. *Adu. Val.*, *passim*); cf. Cyprian's rejection of *tinctio*.

[3] Koffmane, p. 67, states that *condere* is used by Cyprian for *creare*. He does not give a reference, and I have noticed no instance, except *conditor* in *Ep* 75 (824. 12).

[4] *Lex* is used both generally for God's commandments and, in the Scriptural

true reading in 736. 11, and not Hartel's *perscriptio*; cf. 373. 17.

§ 3. Cyprian's characteristic words for God's bearing to men are *censura, dignatio, indulgentia, bonitas*, and *pietas*. *Bonitas* always and *pietas* almost always—perhaps 388. 12, 19 are the only exceptions—are used of Divine goodness, not of human.

Censura may imply either approval (252. 6, &c.) or condemnation, e. g. 670. 14, which is more usual. It is also often used in a general sense, meaning little more than majesty, as in 682. 14, 413. 22, in which it is coupled with *maiestas*, according to Cyprian's usual practice of combining synonyms [1]. *Dignatio* is one of the most common of Cyprian's words. especially in the alliterative phrase *de Dei dignatione*. As a rule it is rather equivalent to favour than to grace, though it describes internal as well as external gifts, e. g. 275. 6. 656. 15, and 716. 23 *benigna et larga d. corda inluminat*. But more commonly it is used of some visible mark of favour, as the episcopate, 546. 19, 651. 9, 671. 20 and often, confessorship or martyrdom, 251. 16, 673. 14, 695. 6, or other Divine

---

sense, for the Old Testament. Beside many classical uses (271. 14, 293. 20, 302. 1, 304. 9, &c.), it is curiously employed, followed by a genitive, in such passages as 285. 11 *ad altare uenire cum simplici corde, cum lege iustitiae, cum concordiae pace*. The two last are paraphrased just afterwards by the simple *iustitia* and *pax*. So 232. 21 in *Dei timore, in lege iustitiae, in dilectione, in opere fides nulla est*, 336. 27 *Deo innocentiae lege deuoti*. In these and in many more passages *lex* seems simply superfluous. In 218. 25 *qui se praepositos sine ulla ordinationis lege constituunt* there is a very Cyprianic equivalent for *ordinatio legitima*. *Legitimus* in Cyprian has not only this meaning of lawful, but also that of appointed by law; 338. 11 *numerus legitimus et certus*, 292. 12 *legitima ad precem tempora*. It comes to mean genuine; 760. 16 *legitimi Christiani*, 762. 8 *legitima fides*, 708. 10 *legitima sanctificatio (sacrificii)*.

[1] *Censura*, which is very frequent, is used of Bishops and others in several senses. The most usual is that of judicial strictness, e. g. 668. 22; also of jurisdiction, or the right to judge, as 189. 20; of obedience to discipline, or loyalty, 625. 15, &c.; of reproof administered, as 623. 18, or sentence passed, as 758. 2. Once at least it is used in a bad sense, 639. 2 *uel duritiae uel censurae suae obstinatione*. In the sense of severity it is used by Tert., and is common in the Hist. Aug. except Vopiscus (Krebs, *Rhein. Mus.* 1892, p. 48).

248 The Style and Language of St. Cyprian.

help, 346. 5, 422. 13, 500. 9, 13, 801. 15. A partial converse is *diuina indignatio* 363. 19, 521. 16. The word is not used of human action. *Indulgentia* occurs constantly in the two senses, both found in Tertullian, of favour and goodness, e. g. 579. 3, 432. 14, in which it is often interchangeable with *dignatio*, as 656. 12 *plebs cui de diuina indulgentia praesumus*, and of forgiveness, e. g. 403. 5 *indulgentia criminis*, 249. 21, 628. 12, &c.

§ 4. *Sermo Dei* is constant, though Tertullian wavers between *Sermo* and *Verbum*. The rendering in Cyprian's version of the Bible seems always to have been *Sermo*. *Concarnatio* occurs once, 60. 5; *incarnatio* never, though *incarnatus* is found in Novatian, *Trin.* 19. Koffmane, p. 42, only knows Hilary of Poitiers as using *concarnatio* in this sense. It was perhaps an unsuccessful coinage of Cyprian. *In uno omnes ipse portauit*, 271. 13, describes the work of the Incarnation; so also 277. 2, 711. 12, 754. 8; cf. Is. 63. 9. Tertullian does not use the phrase; cf. p. 308. *Aduentus* is used both of the first and second Coming, 211. 8, 414. 21, &c. *Passio*[1] 471. 2, and *resurrectio*, are of course common. *Adscensus*, never *adscensio*, is used, 471. 17, &c.

Christus is much more common than *Dominus* or compound titles; the full *Dominus noster Iesus Christus* is very rare; *Dominus Iesus* only occurs in the solemn salutation at the end of the last letter, 842. 9. *Deus et Christus eius*, which occurs so often (see Hartel's *Index Verborum*, s. v. *ellipsis* and *is*, and add 838. 15), may have been misunderstood by Cyprian, as Hartel suggests, for an ellipse of *filius*[2].

Saluare[3] is only used thrice, 790. 20, 809. 6, 12, *Saluator*

---

[1] *Passio* is often used of the martyrs, 578. 2, &c., and in the plural as well as in the singular, e. g. 662. 22, 833. 9.

[2] See a good article on this *eius* by F. Piper in *Zschr. für Kirchengesch.* 1890, p. 67. In Tertullian I have only noticed one instance, in *Bapt.* 9 (208. 19 Reiff.).

[3] Cf. Wölfflin in *Sitzungsberichte* of the Munich Academy, 1893, p. 263 f. *Saluator* is used by the illiterate Celerinus, 529. 12. Tertullian rejects it, though it stood in his Bible, and is constant in Irenaeus. Cyprian never uses Tertullian's *salutificator*, for which add *Marc.* 5. 15 to Oehler's list.

once, 60. 12. These are passages in which Cyprian is making no attempt at style. In rhetorical passages he twice uses *sospitare*, 188. 25, 211. 9; see p. 196. *Seruare* occurs 214. 19, 505. 15, and cf. 319. 20; *reseruare* 373. 13, 640. 20, *conseruare* 279. 15, and *conseruator* 827. 17, as in Tert. *Res. Carn.* 58 *fin.*, *Cult. Fem.* 1. 3. *Saluus fieri* is used occasionally, e. g. 751. 16, 809. 11; *saluus atque incolumis* 367. 10; *Domino et Deo nostro Salutari* 614. 8, the only instance of this Biblical use (Rönsch, *It. V.* p. 100). Cyprian uses *Mediator* only in 60. 19. The Biblical *redemptio* and *Redemptor* are used, e. g. 188. 23, 639. 15, 713. 8, and also *redimere*, e. g. 370. 16; but the verb is commonly employed of human effort by alms, &c., as in 195. 24, 377. 9. Other expressions for the Saviour's work are *peccata portare* 401. 13, 711. 13[1], *remittere* constantly[2], *donare* 249. 21, &c.; *curare, emundare, purgare*, are used indifferently of Divine and human action. *Reparare* 370. 22, 394. 9, &c., *reconciliare Deo* 370. 17 also occur. *Aduocatus* is frequent; *aduocatus et deprecator* occurs twice, 499. 18, 637. 7[3]. *Iudicium* is rarely further described; *cognitio* is an occasional variant. The two are combined 659. 5. *Retributio*, as the

[1] From Is. 53. 4 (*Test.* 2. 13, p. 77, 20). The same reading is in Aug. *C. D.* 18. 29 (Dombart, ed. 2, ii. 295. 6).

[2] The corresponding substantive is *remissa* or *remissio*. The former occurs 19 times, I think, the latter 14 times, in Cyprian's own writing. The latter stood in the African Baptismal question (e. g. 756. 14), and it is usually when speaking directly of this formula that Cyprian uses it, yet not always; cf. 250. 3. The neuter pl. *remissa* (cf. Weyman in Wolfflin's *Archiv* 9. 138), though it has important MS. support, is not likely to be Cyprianic. In the *Sententiae* and in *Ep.* 73 *remissio* is the usual form. This differentiation of form, combined with the constant African use of *saeculum* for the *mundus* which still stood in the Baptismal Service, and was used, though rarely, by Cyprian, shows that Christianity must have been of some considerable antiquity in Africa when Cyprian wrote. These and other differences from the language of the parent Church in Italy must have required the lapse of several generations, especially since they arose between Churches only three days' journey apart.

[3] Mr. H. J. White regards *deprecator* in these passages as equivalent to *propitiator*, since in 1 John 2. 2 (637. 11) ἱλασμός is translated by *deprecatio*, as is ἐξιλασμός in the Vulgate (i. e. O. L.) Sap. 18. 21; but it would be more in accordance with the style of Cyprian that the two words should be practically synonyms.

250 The Style and Language of St. Cyprian.

result of judgment, is reward, 344. 18, &c.; the only exception I have noted is 399. 15. *Vindicta* for punishment is common.

§ 5. There is no variant for *Spiritus Sanctus*. The *sanctus* is rarely omitted, 204. 10, 301. 17, &c., and rarely precedes, though this is contrary to Cyprian's custom. *Praedicere* and *praedicare* occur constantly, the latter as a substitute for *euangelizare*, which Cyprian never uses. There seems to be no clear instance of *praedicare* wrongly used for *praedicere*. *Denuntiare* is used in the same sense 217. 14. For the Divine fulfilment of Scripture the Biblical *adimplere* is used [1].

Inspiratio and *reuelatio*, e. g. 787. 15, where both occur, are common; *adspirare* 841. 10. *Ostensio, ostendere* are used of the giving of visions, e.g. 497. 9, 498. 9, 651. 7. Where *ostendere* is used without the mode of revelation being named, as in 567. 21, it is safe to assume that a vision is implied [2]. *Visio* also is found, e. g. 734. 8. *In Spiritu* occurs 692. 10, &c.; *in ecstasi* only 520. 7 [3]. *Canere* and *praecanere*, both from Tertullian, occur several times, e. g. 375. 19, 706. 13; *diuino spiritu et instinctu*, 359. 6, is used of prophetic inspiration. *Instinctus* [4] in this sense occurs again 255. 16; *instigare* 656. 15, 698. 22. *Spiritus confessionis* is read 338. 26, *spiritus diuinitatis* 339. 26.

§ 6. It will be most convenient here to deal with Cyprian's language concerning Scripture, which he so often attributes to the Holy Spirit [5]. The singular *Scriptura* is much more

---

[1] Add to Hartel's list 225. 6; in different senses 255. 15, 256. 15, 776. 1.

[2] *Ostendere* is so used *Pass. Perp.* §§ 4, 7, 8.

[3] *Pass. Perp.* 20 *adeo in spiritu et in extasi fuerat*. The word is used by Tertullian. In *Ep.* 75 (817. 4) *mulier in ecstasin constituta* it cannot be an ablative, as Koffmane (p. 36) would have it. It must be a rendering of εἰς ἔκστασιν πεσοῦσα, or something similar.

[4] But *instinctus* is more often to evil; 421. 11, 588. 9, 645. 12. *Instinguere*, though used by Tertullian, never occurs in Cyprian.

[5] Cyprian's mode of citation is very uniform. He almost always uses two synonymous verbs in his love of pleonasm; *Deus, Christus, Spiritus Sanctus, Apostolus loquitur et dicit*. In *Ep.* 68 occur the forms *docens et praecipiens, ponit et dicit, docens et ostendens* (twice), *loquens et dicens, mandauit et dixit, ostenditur et probatur, contestatur et dicit, probat et declarat, loquitur et dicit*,

The Language of St. Cyprian. 251

common than *Scripturae*. The standing epithets are *sancta* and *diuina*; *sacra* does not occur. Variants are very rare; *caelestes Scripturae* 254. 9, *dominicae* 538. 5. The other names for Scripture in Cyprian are *disciplina*[1] (*d. caelestis* 287. 25), *lectio*, which clearly has this meaning in 270. 20, 318. 11, 430. 16 (*sit in manibus diuina lectio*), and elsewhere; *libri spiritales* 36. 19; *Scripturae ueteres et nouae* 36. 18, 375. 17. *Testamentum* and *instrumentum* in this sense do not occur. More general terms are *praecepta* 101. 11, 238. 17, &c., and *magisteria*[2], which is very common, and probably derived from the Old Latin New Testament; cf. 193. 6, 522. 15, 738. 16, and especially 505. 15. These words are used with a great wealth of epithets, *diuinus, spiritalis, caelestis, sanctus, salutaris, uitalis, euangelicus*. The legal term *capitula* is used for verses or sections of Scripture, 36. 2, 220. 8, 318. 10, as in Tertullian, but Tertullian's *tituli* is absent.

In the Old Testament *Lex* is not only used alone, but once at least with the genitive of a part; *lex Exodi* 217. 9. Tertullian's *Arithmi* and *Critae* have disappeared, but in the *Testimonia* the true reading is *in Basilion primo*, &c., as against Hartel's *A*, which has almost always *Regnorum*. But elsewhere *Basilion* is not found in the writings of Cyprian; one among many evidences that that work was compiled before Cyprian had settled upon his vocabulary. He uses instead *Regnorum*, or else, and more often, avoids naming the book. Similarly in 142. 3, 329. 7, the only passages where they are named, we read *apud, in Paralipomenon*. The same

---

declarat dicens, addidit dicens, scribit et dicit. Cf. in *Ep.* 74. 3 *clamat et dicit, increpans et obiurgans ponit et dicit, commonet et instruit dicens.* In 425. 20 *Apostolus Paulus instruens et monens ut ... scribit et dicit.* The instances are very rare where Cyprian is content with the simple *Scriptura dicit* or an equivalent.

[1] If Wölfflin in his *Archiv*, viii. p. 11, is right; cf. 468. 1, 230. 5. In all these instances the meaning might be the usual one, yet certainly in Firm. Mat. *De Err.* 19. 5 *quid nobis tradat euangelica disciplina* means Scripture.

[2] Cf. Rendel Harris, *Cod. Sangall.* p. 25. In that MS. *magisterium uel doctrina* occurs as the rendering of διδασκαλία. He compares Irenaeus, 3. 14. 3.

252 The Style and Language of St. Cyprian.

ellipse occurs 338. 8, and often in the *Testimonia*, with *Basiliou* and *Regnorum*. *In Paroemiis* is the regular mode of citation for the book of Proverbs; *in Prooemiis*, 62. 3, can only be a *lapsus calami*. There is some little evidence for *in Parabolis*, 62. 3, 154. 4, though it is not likely to be Cyprian's. Very often the book is included with the other sapiential books, as *in Sapientia*, e. g. 128. 13, 156. 17. In 672. 22 the Minor Prophets are cited collectively; *in duodecim prophetis*. Cf. Tert. *adu. Marc.* 4. 13 *Naum ex duodecim*, and *Adu. Jud.* 5. The other names of books offer nothing noteworthy [1], unless it be that he has *Malachin* (nom. and acc.) twice, 293. 13, 413. 17, and perhaps also 94. 22, *Malachiel* twice at least, 68. 3, 138. 19, against *Malachias* thrice certainly (50. 7, 114. 16, 157. 15), and probably also in 97. 3.

Euangelium [2] is, with one exception, used in the singular, the Gospels being regarded as an undivided whole. Except in the *Testimonia* the form employed is *Dominus in Euangelio suo dicit*, &c., the personal agency of the Evangelists being ignored. In the *Testimonia*, where more exact citation had to be given, *Euangelium cata Matthaeum*, &c. is the description. The evidence for *secundum* is inadequate, and its use improbable [3]. Cyprian never follows Tertullian in speaking of *Euangelium Matthaei*, &c. *Euangelia quattuor*, the only example of the plural, occurs 785. 20. *Acta*, not *Actus*, *Apostolorum* is always used.

Cyprian is very careful not to cite Scripture without acknowledgement. He never allows himself, as does Tertullian, to fall into continuous Scripture language without giving

---

[1] Koffmane, p. 10, notes that *psalmus* is very often used in Cyprian for a verse of a psalm. But when Cyprian writes *psalmus dicit*, &c. he simply personifies the single Psalm, as he does when he writes *Apocalypsis dicit* 342. 21, 663. 5. He recognized them as separate compositions; in the *Testimonia* he gives the number, and his usual citation is *in Psalmis*.

[2] Beside this normal use of *euangelium*, *euangelicus*, it is also used for the Faith as a whole, and practically as an equivalent for *ecclesia*, e. g. 248. 26 *nec ecclesiae iungitur qui ab euangelio separatur*, 687. 3 *sacerdos Dei euangelium tenens*, cf. 544. 12.

[3] Cf. Zahn, *Neutest. Kanon*, I. 164, n. 5.

The Language of St Cyprian. 253

notice of the fact. The only instances where short passages are quoted without warning are, so far as I have observed, 228. 23, 290. 21, 379. 21, 507. 7, 711. 2. Beside *Dominus &c. dicit, Scriptura* is frequently personified as the speaker. The impersonal *inquit* appears occasionally, e. g. 738. 18, 23; and similarly *quando occurrat dicens* 668. 23; for these cf. Miodoński's note to *De Aleatt.* p. 61.

§ 7. Cyprian had frequent occasion to show that the facts of the Christian Faith are foreshown in the Old Testament. For type he appears only once to use *mysterium* 86. 6; *typus* often, e. g. 269. 11, 386. 25, 704. 11, but, with his usual dislike of Greek words, more often *imago*, e. g. 189. 14, 367. 16, 702. 24, or *figura*, as 217. 10, 705. 2. Once *instar* occurs, 785. 17; *umbra et imago* 328. 4, 719. 25; *praefiguratio* 763. 14; *signum et sacramentum* 216. 13, 330. 19; *sacramentum* [1]

---

[1] As this is the first occasion on which I have to refer to this word, I will here try to classify its uses in Cyprian. This is not easy, as the various meanings often overlap, and the word in many instances was used with intentional vagueness. It is used twice of the military oath; 246. 12 *sacramenti mei memor deuotionis et fidei arma suscepi*; and 806. 4. Of loyalty to that oath, 491. 21 *spectaculum quam sublime ... quam Dei oculis sacramento et deuotione militis eius acceptum.* In a very common sense it comes to mean a *bond*, however it may have attained the meaning; e. g. 754 15 *inseparabile unitatis s.*, 215. 7 *unitas sacramentis caelestibus cohaerens*; ib. 11 *unitatis s., uinculum concordiae*, which are identical phrases; so also 639 5 *manente concordiae uinculo et perseuerante catholicae ecclesiae sacramento*; 668. 8 *copulati sacramento unanimitatis.* The action of heretics, &c. on this bond is described 241. 21 as *soluere*, 808. 22 *inpugnare*, 794. 10 *mutilare*, 227. 19 *disturbare.* Also a rule or law, as 600. 4 s. *semel traditum diuinae dispositionis et catholicae unitatis*, cf. 551. 8 (Novatian). A doctrine, sometimes with the connotation of mystery, e g. 36. 13 *item libellus alius continet Christi s., quod idem u'nerit qui adnuntiatus est* sq , *Test.* 3 50 *tit. s. fidei non esse profanandum*; ib 2 2 *tit de sacramento concarnationis eius et passionis* sq.; 288. 1 *sic cum doceret quid sit uita aeterna s. uitae magna et diuina breuitate conplexus est*; 710 2, 713. 9, &c. Similarly in *Ep.* 77 (834. 7) Nemesianus says *dum non desinis occulta sacramenta nudare.* From this meaning it seems to be extended to that of lesson generally; 272. 8 *qualia sunt dominicae orationis sacramenta, quam magna* sq. From the meaning of mystery comes that of type, in which mysterious teaching is conveyed; this is very common, e. g. 292. 6, 13, 337 27, 764 8, 808 23, &c.; of symbolical action in 83. 12 *sacramento unctionis Christum significans*; an instance or example 763. 13; cf. 702. 14 *Christus ... qui scripturarum omnium sacramento ac testimonio*

254 The Style and Language of St. Cyprian.

alone very often. The verbs used are *typum, figuram,* &c. *exprimere* 702. 24, &c., which is the most common; *gerere* 386. 26; *portare* 269. 11; *praemonstrare* 704. 12; *ostendere* 702. 23. The type as representing its antitype is said *designare*; 752. 21 *qui agnus designabat Christum*; *praeformare* 217. 4[1], *exprimere* 338. 25, *praefigurare* 328. 5, *initiare* 403. 27, *Abel passionem Christi initians,* and 285. 13. *Veritas,* as in 367. 16, 702. 23, and *respondere,* as 593. 21, stand for the antitype.

§ 8. *Christianus* is common, but less common than might have been expected. It is rare as an adjective, *Christianum nomen* 211. 15, *patientia* 404. 15, *unanimitas* 754. 4, and a few more. When used as a substantive it always seems to have the connotation of a good Christian, and to be reserved for somewhat emphatic passages. *Fidelis,* on the other hand, is a colourless term; cf. in *Test.* 3. the titles §§ 34, 37, 44, 57, 87. Caldonius can use it even of lapsed persons, 537. 4; Tertullian *Fug.* 1 includes renegades under the term, and *Jeiun.* 11 contrasts it with *Spiritalis,* i. e. Montanist. Similarly *fides* appears to be used simply for the fact of Baptism in *Test.* 3. 11 *tit. eum qui fidem consecutus est,* and *ib.* 97 *tit.,* as in Tertullian *Monog.* 11 *maritus a fide primus,* and *Pud.* 18 [2].

praedicetur, i. e. witness both typical and direct. In 710. 23 it appears to mean not the type but the teaching which it conveys. The word is used frequently in the modern meaning of sacrament; e.g. *baptismi s.* 795. 24; *s. salutare* (i. e. Baptism) 761. 2; *si sacramento utroque nascantur* (i. e. Baptism and *manus impositio*) 775. 16, 795. 12, and *Sent.* 5 (439. 9). So of the Eucharist, 431. 17 *de sacramento crucis et cibum et potum sumis*; and even of the elements, 255. 19 *diaconus reluctanti licet de sacramento calicis infudit,* where *de* is partitive; 'poured some of the sacrament of the cup into the child's mouth.' It is used also of the Passover; *sacramentum Paschae* 217. 8, 752. 20; and of means of grace generally, 770. 19. In 370. 19 *hunc si fieri potest, sequamur omnes, huius sacramento et signo censeamur,* it seems to mean the sign of the Cross; cf. 664. 25. In *Sent.* 7 (440. 19) it is equivalent to *Symbolum.*

[1] Cf. *forma facti* = τύποι γενόμενοι in the Vg. of 1 Pet. 5. 3, and *deformare* in this sense in Tert. *Res. Carn.* 30.

[2] This distinction seems the best explanation of *Christiani fideles,* which occurs seven times in the probably Cyprianic *De Spect*, *fidelis* being the substantive and of *Christiana fidelis,* Tert. *Ux.* 2. 8, i. e. a baptized person

Christians are often called simply *nostri*, 301. 7, 522. 14, &c. *Homo Dei* occurs six times, 365. 12, &c., *homo Dei et Christi* 297. 13; *seruus Dei* is common. They are called *diuinum genus* 366. 22, and are contrasted with *genus humanum* 301. 15[1]. *Credentes* is very common, as is *fidentes* 510. 19, &c., probably invented by Cyprian as a stronger cognate term for the weak *fideles*; it does not appear to be used by Tertullian. *Creduli* is absent, though the negative is common[2].

§ 9. *Ecclesia*[3] is often paraphrased by *domus Dei*, e.g. 477. 4, 674. 24, or *domus fidei* 300. 19, 777. 20, &c. *Ecclesia quae catholica una est* 733. 9, and fairly often, e. g. 597. 13. Cyprian does not use the elliptic *Catholica*, sc. *ecclesia*, of Cornelius (611. 16). The epithet *sancta*[4], 767. 9, seems to have no variant, and is not very common. Cornelius writes (611. 8) *sanctissima catholica ecclesia*[5]. The Church is frequently said to be *aedificata* or *fundata super Petrum*. This occurs 194. 25, 212. 14 (the famous passage in *De Un.* 4), 338. 17, 403. 16,

worthy of the name of Christian; cf. A. 4. 17 *homo Christianus fidelis*, where both are epithets. In *De Rebapt.* 11 (A 83. 5) *nihil interest utrum hic uerbum audiens an fidelis sit qui confitetur Dominum* the words simply mean unbaptized or baptized; cf. *fidei sacramentum* = Baptism in Tert. *De. An.* 1 (299 22 Reiff).

[1] *Quoadusque istic in mundo sumus cum genere humano carnis aequalitate coniungimur, spiritu separamur.* It would add point to Tacitus' *odium generis humani* if it were a recognized term by which the Christians distinguished the heathen from themselves; and might seem consistent with the charge of magic brought against them under the same name; cf. Ramsay, *The Church in the Roman Empire*, p. 236. Yet in 393. 26, 404. 26, 409. 15 *genus humanum* is used inclusively; in 306. 12 *sine ullo discrimine generis humani* it seems to be used of heathen not being selected for punishment in this world.

[2] *Credulitas* = *fides* is not employed by Cyprian, but by Nemesianus, 834. 8, which seems the earliest instance. Cyprian has it in a bad sense 210. 4, 731. 7. It recurs in Arnobius and Jerome for *fides*. *Incredulus, incredulitas, infidelis* are common.

[3] The exact phrase *extra ecclesiam nulla salus*, often attributed to Cyprian, does not occur in his writings. The nearest approach to it is 795. 3 *salus extra ecclesiam non est*, and 477. 5.

[4] Here may be noted the rarity of *sacer*: 688. 2 *cleri nostri sacer uenerandusque congestus* is almost the only instance; the word is avoided in an obvious antithesis 724. 12.

[5] *Catholicus* is not used so widely as in Tertullian; *catholica regula* 767. 3, *fides* 538. 20, *catholicae institutionis unitas* 604. 11, and a few more.

594. 6 ¹, 674. 16, 732. 25, 769. 20, 773. 12, 783. 15. *Petra* is so used in *Ep.* 75 (820. 27, cf. 821. 16), but never by Cyprian. In 338. 17 Hartel has introduced it into the text on insufficient MS. authority, and in spite of Cyprian's constant use of *super Petrum*. For the description of faithful Christians as *super petram fundati*, see § 24. In connexion with the Church, Cyprian also often uses the words *matrix, radix, origo, caput*; e g. 607. 9 *ut ecclesiae catholicae matricem et radicem agnoscerent ac tenerent*, 808. 2 *caput et origo*, 779. 19 *caput et radix*, 772. 23. &c. *ueritas et matrix* ², 600. 2 *radix et mater*. How far *matrix* is equivalent to *mater* it is difficult to say; in 607. 9 the word was probably chosen for the rhyme; cf. 214. 14, 338. 15. *Ecclesia sponsa Christi* (*Test.* 2. 19 *tit.*) is carried out as a metaphor with great consistency, e. g. 804. 21 *apud solam sponsam Christi quae parere spiritaliter et generare filios Deo possit*, 243. 15 *ecclesiam matrem, patrem Deum*, and even more strongly 214. 17 ff. *Ecclesia mater* is of constant occurrence, 490. 5, 588 13, &c. In 680. 23 *matris sinus* is opposed to *nouerca*. Heresy is *adulterium* 214. 17, 667. 2, &c. *Corrumpere, uiolare*, &c. were certainly used by Cyprian much more literally in this connexion than we, with our ways of thinking, should assume; cf. especially 593. 21. *Adunare* (usually the perfect participle) and *adunatio* are often used of the Church, 238. 10, 620. 3, 698. 21, &c. *Intus* and *foris* express membership and exclusion; *plebs intus posita* 687. 17, *foris esse* 745. 9; both together 732. 13 f. But the pleonastic *intus in ecclesia, foris extra ecclesiam* is much more common; 784. 20, 214. 25, &c. Except this last example, from *De Un.* 6, it is confined to the

---

[1] In this passage *una cathedra* is joined with *una ecclesia*; cf. 630. 2, 683. 10.

[2] The following list is, I think, a complete one of the passages in which one or more of these words occur in connexion with the Church; 188. 9, 212. 3, 213. 1, 214. 4, 14, 220. 24, 231. 11, 338. 15, 403. 26, 404. 2, 579. 9, 701. 22, 769. 20, 783. 14, 786. 23, in addition to those given above. In different contexts cf. 352. 15, 421. 4. In no instance can the use of *matrix* be that of *urbs primaria regionis alicuius* which Paucker in his *Addenda* gives from later writers. Tertullian makes a use of the word similar to Cyprian's, but wider.

The Language of St. Cyprian. 257

Baptismal controversy, where it occurs at least fourteen times. *Foris seorsum* is used 672. 9, *foris positi et extra ecclesiam constituti* 778. 13 ; cf. 785. 17.

Ecclesia is of course used for the local as well as for the universal Church ; *ecclesiae omnes* 627. 11, *ecclesia principalis* (Rome) 683. 10, &c., yet Cyprian does not often use the word in this sense.

The body of Christians is occasionally *secta* ; 101. 8 *quaedam capitula* (of Scripture) *ad religiosam sectae nostrae disciplinam pertinentia* ; 543. 8 *moderatus et cautus et humilitate ac timore sectae nostrae uerecundus*. In 397. 8 *uiis quibus ad consequenda diuinitus praemia spei ac fidei nostrae secta dirigitur* there is a violent enallage (for many similar cf. Koziol, *Der Stil des L. Apuleius*, p. 223 f.). But this use of *secta* is much more common in Tertullian.

§ 10. Lay members of the Church are *laici* 632 6, &c., but not very often ; usually *plebs* or *populus*. Of these two *plebs* is the less common ; *plebs cui praesumus* 656. 12, *ea plebs cui praepositus ordinatur* 739. 10 ; *stantium plebs* 526. 6, &c. *Plebs Domini, Christi* is an inclusive term for all Christians, 219. 6, 390. 5, &c. Once the plural occurs, 735. 9 *plebes consistentes ad Legionem et Asturicae*, of the lay members of the communities. *Populus*[1] *credentium, Christianorum, ecclesiae, noster* (211. 14, 363. 1, 414. 25, 730. 15, 732. 12, &c.) is very frequent. It also stands alone, e. g. 239. 16 *populi aliquando numerosi multiplex iactura*; cf. *Sent*. 33 (449. 1) *nec duobus populis salutarem aquam tribuere potest ille qui unius gregis pastor est*. *Populus*, but not *plebs*, is used of the heathen as well as of Christians, e. g. 390. 5, where *populus perditionis ac mortis* is opposed to *plebs Christi*, 711. 3, &c.

§ 11. The four terms, *episcopus, sacerdos, antistes, praepositus* are used for *Bishop*. The first three have only this one sense. *Episcopus* (*coepiscopus, pseudoepiscopus, episcopatus*) is not much

---

[1] Sittl, *Lokale Verschiedenheiten*, p. 108, is right in saying that *populi* in the vulgar sense is absent from Cyprian. In the sense of *multitudo* it occurs occasionally, 314. 1, 343. 6 ; 581. 4 *populus circumstans* = *circumstantes*.

258 The Style and Language of St. Cyprian.

more common than *sacerdos*. The latter (with *sacerdotium, consacerdos, sacerdotalis*), though no doubt it is often used because the name involved an argument and a claim, is employed so freely and so naturally that it must have been a current term of unmistakable import [1]. *Antistes* used, like

---

[1] In Cyprian's writings there is no passage where *sacerdos* must, and not many where it can, be equivalent to *presbyter*. The numerous cases where *episcopi et sacerdotes* occurs are simply pieces of Cyprianic rhetoric, like *preces et orationes, aduersarius et inimicus = diabolus*, and many more, cf. p. 230. In *Ep.* 1 (466. 16) the decree of *episcopi antecessores nostri* is called in 467. 4 *sacerdotum decretum*. In *Ep.* 15. 1 (514. 3) *sacerdos Dei* is contrasted with *presbyteri*; cf. 522. 4. The Church of Carthage has only one *sacerdos*; 581. 12 *ut Domini misericordia plebi suae sacerdotem reddat incolumem*. The bishop's seat is *cathedra sacerdotalis* 630. 2. Other passages where the same meaning is obvious are *Ep.* 3, throughout which *episcopus* and *sacerdos* are interchangeable, *Ep.* 55. 9, and '*Ep.* 67. 2. There are, I think, only five passages where *presbyter* can be the meaning of *sacerdos*; (1) *singuli diuino sacerdotio honorati et in clerico ministerio constituti*, which includes all the clergy : *diuino* makes it likely that presbyters are embraced in the sacerdotium; cf. the reference to 629. 9 in my note, p. 260. (2) 586. 6 f. the *presbyter* Numidicus was all but slain in the persecution, and survived against his will ; *remansit inuitus, sed remanendi, ut uidemus, haec fuit causa ut eum clero nostro Dominus adiungeret et desolatam per lapsum quorundam presbyterorum nostrorum copiam gloriosis sacerdotibus adornaret. et promouebitur quidem* sq. This might mean that Carthage, which has lost presbyters, shall be provided with fresh ones ; but it is much more probable that the sense is that the Church which has lost mere presbyters shall have the honour of a bishop being elected from among its clergy. This explains *et promouebitur quidem*, which the other translation does not. (3) 697. 1 *et cum episcopo presbyteri sacerdotali honore coniuncti*; here *honor* must not be pressed. *Licentia* or *potestas* is never attributed to presbyters. It refers to the outward respect paid to them as in *Test.* 3. 85, 465. 5, 585. 14, 689. 13. (4) 738. 20 *nec hoc in episcoporum tantum et sacerdotum sed et in diaconorum ordinationibus obseruasse apostolos animaduertimus*. Here again the words are identical. There is no such formal record in the Book of Acts of the ordination of presbyters as there is of that of St Matthias and of the Seven. (5) 777. 1 *oportet enim sacerdotes et ministros qui ulturi et sacrificus deseruiunt integros adque inmaculatos esse*. Here O. Ritschl, *Cyprian u. d. Verfassung d. Kirche*, p. 231, would translate *presbyters and deacons*. But in *Laps.* 6 (240. 16) *sacerdotes* and *ministeria* (or perhaps *ministri*) include the whole clergy, and may do so here. Cyprian is always a careless writer, and it would not be well to press this single instance. He is no doubt referring directly to presbyters and deacons (776. 15), but has used the other terms as an argument *a fortiori*. O. Ritschl, *l. c.*, cites Huther as denying that *sacerdos* in Cyprian means *presbyter*. In Tertullian, Kolberg, *Verfassung, &c. d. Kirche nach d. Schr. Tertullians*, p. 41, fails to give a clear instance of *sacerdos = presbyter* ; yet the argument of the famous passage

sacerdos, of the Priests of the Old Testament (*Zacharias antistes Dei* 687. 5, *Z. sacerdos* 337. 5) is used frequently of bishops, and of no others; 254. 4 *antistites et sacerdotes* pleonastic, like *episcopi et sacerdotes*, and so Min. Fel. 9. 4. *Praepositus* normally means a bishop; 729. 20 *omnes praepositos qui apostolis uicaria ordinatione succedunt*, 218. 25, 765. 24, &c.; *praepositi et sacerdotes* pleonastic, 730. 8. In 470. 5 Aaron is *sacerdos praepositus*. But in 514. 18 *praepositi* are the clergy in the absence of the bishop, as in the Roman *Ep.* 8 (486. 6) *praepositi et uice pastorum* during the vacancy of the see. In 475. 15 *praepositi et diaconi* are synonyms; cf. Tert. *Fug.* 11, where *praepositi* is used inclusively for the whole *clerus*. *Pastor*, e. g. *Test.* 1. 14 *tit.* and *gubernator*, e. g. 674. 1 are also frequently used, and of bishops only. In *Ep.* 66. 5 Cyprian describes himself by all these six titles, *episcopus, praepositus, pastor, gubernator, antistes, sacerdos* (730. 10). He uses *caput* in 600. 6; cf. 203. 6.

Bishops are *collegae* and form a *collegium*. There seems no reason to suppose that *antecessor* (466. 16, &c.) has any other sense in Cyprian than the temporal, cf. the common *successio*, though Koffmane, p. 58, suggests that it conveys the notion of authority as well, and is derived from the Jurists[1]. The latter may well be the case. *Locus, gradus,* and *cathedra*, all of frequent occurrence, are used of the bishop's position. His authority is usually described as *licentia* or *potestas*, words only used of bishops.

§ 12. *Presbyter* (*presbyterium*, both collective and of the

in *Exh. Cast.* 7 requires, or at least gains strength from, the identity in meaning of these terms. Ambrose in his *Epp.*, and the documents included in that collection, consistently use *sacerdos* = *episcopus*. Schepss in Wolfflin's *Archiv*, 3. 323, notes the same of Priscillian; see also Mioduński's note to *De Aleatt.* p. 62, with his references. Jerome is the earliest writer to waver in the matter, often using *sacerdos* in both senses, as does Augustine. who states, *C. D.* 20. 10 (Dombart, ed. 2, ii. 433. 16) that the name belongs to both Orders. As late as Ps.-Ignatius, *Hero*, § 3, and Ps.-Pionius, *Vita Polyc.* § 21, ἱερεύς is used without qualification for 'bishop.' Cyprian constantly calls presbyters his *conpresbyteri*, never his *consacerdotes* or *collegae*. He does not use Tertullian's *summus sacerdos* for 'bishop.'

[1] Cf. Kolberg, *op cit.* p. 38, n 1:.

office, *conpresbyter*) has no variant. In *Test.* 3. 76 *maiorem natu non temere accusandum* Cyprian is bound by his Biblical text (Vg. *presbyterum*). In *Ep.* 75 (814. 30) *maiores natu* is one among many strong evidences against Cyprian as the original translator, as is *seniores* in the same letter, 812. 22.

Diaconus (*diaconium*; for forms see p. 297) is also constant, though it is tempting in a few cases to regard *minister*, *administratio* as meaning 'deacon' and 'diaconate'[1]. For *dia-*

---

[1] Cf. Koffmane, pp. 25, 150. *Minister* and its cognates are often used, and in various senses, by Cyprian. In 590. 15 the clergy other than the bishop are classed as *presbyteri, diaconi, cetera ministeria*; 465. 11 *singuli diuino sacerdotio honorati et in clerico ministerio constituti*, where *et* is disjunctive; cf. Tert. *Praescr.* 29 *tot sacerdotia, tot ministeria perperam functa*; *ministri ecclesiae* 571. 1 refers primarily to two subdeacons and an acolyte. In 240 16 the term is inclusive, as also 466. 21. But 738. 25 *altaris ministerium* is 'the office of a deacon,' and the Levites, who are the counterpart to Cyprian of the deacon, are always *ministri* with a *ministerium*, 470. 3, 757. 1, &c; 469. 10 *diaconus officii ac ministerii sui oblitus*. There is a clear example of *minister = clericus*, and probably *diaconus*, in *Ep.* 21 (Celerinus), 531. 12, where the true reading appears to be *et nunc super ipsos factum antistites Dei recognoui idem minister*, ' I, myself a *minister*, recognize you as raised above God's bishops ' By the common notion that orders were bestowed, *ipso facto*, on confessors, Celerinus in his modesty gives himself a lower and his friend a higher grade in the ministry; cf. Hermas, *Vis.* 3. 2, 1, Harnack, *Dogmengesch.* 1 184 n., and the Roman *Ep.* 8 (488. 10), where the confessors precede the presbyters; also Lightfoot, *Apostolic Fathers*, vol. 3. 241. The evidence is stronger for *administratio = diaconatus*. In 2 Cor. 9. 12 διακονία is translated *administratio* in Cyprian's Bible (113 20, 380. 23) instead of the Vulgate *ministerium*; 617 1 *diaconio sanctae administrationis amisso* appears an identical genitive (cf. *preces orationis*, &c., and *apostolatus ducatus* in *De Aleatt.* 1); 590. 14 *diaconi ecclesiasticae administrationi deuoti*. But the word is used of Aaron's office 411. 10, and therefore also of bishops, 489. 3 *integritas administrationis*, 828. 19, &c., as is *administrare*; *sacerdotium Dei administrare* 735. 17, 770. 15, *Sent.* 1 (437. 5); cf. 510. 15, 608. 6. Both *administratio* and *ministerium* are used of the lower orders of the ministry in the twin passages, 581. 22, 588. 2. In 629. 9 *Cornelius . . . per omnia ecclesiastica officia promotus et in diuinis administrationibus Dominum saepe promeritus* implies, I think, that Cornelius had been a presbyter, for except in this one passage *diuinus* (which probably refers to the Eucharist) is confined to *sacerdotium*, *ecclesiasticus* being the only epithet given to the diaconate and lower grades. Tertullian in *Exh Cast.* 10 seems to use *minister* of the celebrant at the altar It is remarkable how little, no doubt intentionally, Cyprian refers to the presbyterate; cf. his avoidance of the word *sacerdos* in relation to it. In another sense *ministerium* occurs 548. 1 *scio . . . paucos (clericos) qui illic sunt uix ad m. cotidianum operis sufficere*, and 502. 12.

conium see p. 299, and cf. Koffmane, p. 25. *Diaconatus* does not occur.

Hypodiaconus is always used for the African subdeacon, not only by Cyprian, but by others, as in *Epp.* 77, 78, 79. It is also used in 572. 12 in a Roman letter, but of a Carthaginian officer. The only case of *subdiaconus* is in the Roman *Ep.* 8 (485. 20); a Carthaginian is spoken of, and this seems the earliest use of the word. No Roman subdeacon is named.

Lector, lectio have no variant; *lectionem dare alicui* 548. 6. *Acoluthus* also is invariable, as is *exorcista*, though Cyprian rejects the verb *exorcizare*. *Proximi clero* 548. 5 suggests the *proximi* of the Roman civil service[1]. Cyprian mentions all orders of the ministry except the deaconess and the *ostiarius*.

For *religio, religiosus* in the sense of orders, clerical, see the note to § 24. *Clerus* as a collective noun is very common, e. g. 466. 10, 689. 13; as an abstract[2] it is absent. *Clericus* is common as a substantive, naturally for the most part in the plural; as an adjective it is rare, *cl. ministerium* 465. 11, *ordinatio* 466. 10, *epistula* 489. 18, &c. The collective *ordo* (e. g. 808. 17) is very rare, though common in Tertullian.

The words normally employed by Cyprian to describe the appointment of clergy are *constituere, ordinare, facere*. All are used of all ranks, e. g. a bishop *electus et constitutus* 608. 8; *Sent.* 78 *non olim sum episcopus constitutus*; of a lector 584. 21. *Ordinare, ordinatio* are the most common, e. g. *delectus diuina ordinatione episcopus* 696. 26; cf. Hartel's *Index Rerum*; it is used of a deacon 738. 21, of a lector 581. 5. *Facere* is not so common; 593. 8, 597. 12, &c. *Deferre episcopatum*

Nemesianus in *Ep* 77 (835 18) actually uses the word for concrete alms; *m quod distribuendum misisti*. The work of the apostles is *ministerium salutis* in 755. 19. In *De Rebapt.* 5 (A 75. 31) *integritas ministerii* = validity of the ministerial act, i. e. Baptism. Hartel need not have doubted the text.

[1] *Proximi memoriae, a memoria*, &c., holding a position between that of a procurator and of his subalterns. Cf. Hirschfeld, *Untersuchungen*, pp. 211, 215, 265, &c.

[2] In such senses as *De Rebapt.* 1 (A. 70. 26) *nullum in quocunque clero constitutum*; yet cf. 741. 9.

262 The Style and Language of St. Cyprian.

alicui occurs 739. 17; *cooptare* 678. 9 and *creare* 642. 22 are only used of heretical bishops. *Eligere* and *deligere* both occur several times. The voice of the laity is always *suffragium* 629. 24, 738, 15. *Manum inponere in episcopatum* 739. 17 and 610. 4 (Cornelius). Deposition from orders is twice described by *deponere*, 472. 6 and 739. 23. Usually he contents himself with the wider term *abstinere*, or such general expressions as *excitare de presbyterio, separare se a peccatore praeposito, indignos recusare* (619. 9, 737. 22, 738. 2), &c.

§ 13. Councils of different kinds are frequently mentioned, but Cyprian appears to avoid anything like technical language concerning their assembly or proceedings. Usually he describes their meeting as *in unum conuenire* 627. 14, 779. 2, or *praesentes adesse* 465. 5, 581. 5; *concilium habere* occurs 628. 6, 677. 20; *concilium agere* 680. 10[1]; *cogere et celebrare concilium* 775. 5. *Conuentus* occurs 600. 22; cf. the *conuenticulum* of heresy 220. 23, &c. It does not come within the scope of this paper to deal with the constitution of these Councils, for there is no distinction in Cyprian's language as to their meeting, their proceedings or their decisions, except that in 465. 4, *ego et collegae mei qui praesentes aderant et conpresbyteri nostri qui nobis adsidebant*, some distinction might seem to be made as to the status of the different Orders. But in 771. 6 *quid nuper in concilio plurimi coepiscopi cum conpresbyteris qui aderant censuerimus*, there seems to be no difference. For the debates of the Council Cyprian has a great wealth of language; *communicato et librato de omnium conlatione consilio* 626. 13, *librata consilii communis examinatione* 717. 16, *ponderare, examinare, pondus examinare, limare, tractare*[2], &c. The de-

---

[1] *Concilio frequenter acto* This must mean frequently assembled, and not largely attended, as the Archbishop of Canterbury would have it in his article *Cyprian* in the *Dict. Chr. Biogr. Frequenter* is Cyprian's usual word for often; he only uses *saepe* for purposes of rhythm, and perhaps not more than twelve times in the whole of his writings. Did *frequenter* mean anything but 'often' in the third century?

[2] Of debates or modes of procedure during the session there is no account. In 627. 16 we read that at a Council of bishops *scripturis diu ex utraque parte*

cision of the council is *decernere, statuere* (*statuere et firmaie* 774. 14), *indicare* or *censere*, all of frequent occurrence. The substantives used for the decisions are *sententia, decretum, placitum,* and once (466. 22) *forma.*

The assembly of the clergy at other times than at a council is *consessus* 586. 15, no doubt of the bishop and presbyters only, and *congestus* (unless this be, as is more probable, the dais on which they sat) 688. 2. So also 585. 2 *sessuri nobiscum* is a promise that a lector shall be advanced to the presbyterate. In 689. 13 *clerus tecum praesidens* includes the whole clergy, and refers to function rather than to dignity.

§ 14. The first stage towards Christianity is named *uenire.* Cyprian, with his dislike of Greek words, never used *proselytus,* though it occurs in Tertullian. In the letters of the Baptismal controversy *uenire, ueniens, ad Christum, ad ecclesiam,* &c. are constant. Occasionally he ventures on *ueniens* alone; 769. 18 *uenientem baptizare. Catecumenus* occurs twice, 106. 18, 795. 16 (i.e. in *Test.* and Baptismal *Epp.*, in which no attention is paid to style), and in the Roman *Ep.* 8 (488 2), *catechista* never, *catechizare* only in *Ep.* 75 (823. 17). *Audiens* is twice used for *catecumenus,* 524. 14, 548. 8 [1], *doctor* for *catechista*; *presbyteri doctores* are mentioned 548. 6, and a *doctor* [2] *audientium* ib. 8, the latter being a lector; *doctor* without further description 780. 20. *Nouus, nouellus, rudis* seem merely descriptive epithets, and not substitutes for the absent *neophytus,* which has been deliberately avoided.

§ 15. Often as Cyprian has to speak about Baptism, he has no such wealth of synonyms as other writers. He does not

---

prolatis temperamentum salubri moderatione librauimus, which must mean a compromise. The use of Scripture suggests that in 523. 4 *ut . . . conuocatis coepiscopis secundum Domini disciplinam . . . martyrum litteras examinaie possimus, disciplina* may mean 'Scripture,' as in certain other passages; cf. § 6.

[1] Cf. *uerbum audiens* in *De Rebapt.* 11, 14 (A 82. 31, 83. 5, 87. 10) = *catecumenus.* Cf. Kolberg, *op. cit.* p. 63.

[2] So Hartel in his *Ind. Rer. s. v. doctores,* though in his text he reads *doctorum,* and in the *Ind. Verb. doctores audientes.* It seems impossible to make sense if the traditional reading *doctorem* be abandoned.

go far beyond Biblical language. It is impossible to make a distinction of meaning between *baptismus* and *baptisma*. For forms see p. 297. *Tinguere, tinctio* are confined to heretical Baptism, except in two passages, 543. 12, 782. 5, where Cyprian is indirectly citing Scripture[1]. The only use of *inluminare* = φωτίζειν in this sense seems to be 789. 12 *quomodo possunt tenebrae inluminare?* where the context suggests Baptism, though it may be only a general expression; cf. *Sent.* 22 (445. 10). *Abluere* occurs occasionally; 752. 6 *baptizandi adque abluendi hominis potestatem*; ib. 3 *ablui et purgari eius lauacro*; 219. 21. This no doubt is from 1 Cor. 6. 11 in Cyprian's Bible (168. 3, 275. 11) as well as the Vulgate. In all other instances it has an object in Cyprian, *crimen, sordes* or similar words[2]. Christians are *recreati et renati* 294. 11, 365. 21, *reparati* 400. 27, &c., *expiati* 6. 4, 8. 5, 751. 16, *innouati* 204. 6, 769. 7, 803. 1; *reformatus in nouum hominem* occurs 803. 8, *redintegrare* 279. 15. *Purificare* 786. 24, &c. is rare; cf. 578. 26. *Regeneratio, sanctificatio, renasci* are common property of Christian writers. Baptism is *natiuitas secunda* 6. 6 and often, *iterata* 204. 7, *caelestis* 427. 28, &c. Other similar epithets are also used; cf. Koffmane, p. 78. It is *lauacrum salutare* 204. 6, &c., *uitale* 188. 14; *aqua uitalis, salutaris* 374. 8, 752. 5; in the rhetorical language of the *Ad Donatum*, 6. 3 *unda genitalis*. *Fons* in 785. 21, &c. is purely metaphorical[3]. For the use of *sacramentum* see the note to § 7, p. 253. Those who are duly baptized

---

[1] This contumelious use of a word which had been normal in the previous generation (Tertullian and the African Bible) must be an indirect attack on Montanism, to which Cyprian never alludes, though it undoubtedly existed in Carthage in his day. *Intinguere*, which also occurs in Tertullian, is used several times in the *Sententiae*, and *tinctio* survived till the sixth century. Paucker, *Subrelicta*, cites it both from Fulg. Rusp. and Fulg. Ferr. In other respects there is little difference between the language of Cyprian and Tertullian concerning Baptism and the Eucharist.

[2] See Wölfflin in his *Archiv*, 4. 569. His earliest instances of *abluere* = *baptizare* are Tert. *adu. Marc.* 1. 14, Iren. 4. 27. 1.

[3] Yet Koffmane, p. 76, sees in it an allusion to a concrete sense of *fons* in Baptism.

become *legitimi Christiani* 760. 16; cf. *legitimi fideles* in *De Rebapt.* 14 (A 87. 12). The gift in Baptism is *gratia*[1], 719. 15, 760. 15, 273. 6, &c. The Baptismal questions are *interrogatio*[2], 756. 10, &c. *Symbolum*, 756. 7, according to Harnack, *Dogmengesch.* I. 103 n., is the earliest use of the word.

Vestigium infantis for *pes*, 719. 13, in the ceremonial kissing of the foot which formed part of the Baptismal rite, is no doubt part of Cyprian's attempt to elevate Christian diction. It appears not to be Biblical. The word attained some currency. In the twenty-third sermon attributed to Fulgentius Ruspensis, *De pedibus lauandis*, it is constantly used of the feet.

Concerning *unctio* and *signum crucis* (*signaculum dominicum* 785. 5, *consignari* 751. 6, *signari* 783. 10, *signum et sacramentum* 370. 19, *signum Dei* 664. 25) nothing need be said. *Chrisma* occurs only 768. 14, and is there explained by *unctio*. *Manus inpositio*, after Baptism and penitence and in Ordination, is constant, though the simple *manus* occurs once at least (248. 22). That it is a single word, as Hartel suggests in his *Index Verborum*, seems clear, in spite of one or two rhetorical postpositions of *manus*[3].

§ 16. The word *Eucharistia* is not very common. It is

---

[1] *Gratia* is less used by Cyprian than might have been expected. Besides this use for the gift in Baptism, which is much the most common, it is used for other gifts or favours, e. g. 293. 7 *aduentus Christi aeternae gratiam lucis praebiturus*, 365. 17 *gratia omnis et copia regni caelestis*, 380. 18 *beatus Paulus dominicae inspirationis gratia plenus*. It seems actually to mean 'reward' in several passages, e.g. 202. 18 *uirgines quarum ad gratiam merces secunda est*, 204. 3, 311. 1, 421. 14, &c. *Gratia Dei* = *bonitas* occurs occasionally, 272. 13, 275. 20, &c.; *gratia et indulgentia* together, 432. 14; 425. 10 *homo ad Dei gratiam pertinens* is a Cyprianic abstraction for *ad Deum*. The word is not often used in a general sense of 'spiritual power bestowed'; yet cf. 260 12, 320. 20. In connexion with the Eucharist I have only noted the strange use, 256. 14 *gratia salutaris in cinerem mutatur* = *hostia*; cf. *ministerium* – *stips* 835. 18.

[2] Beside the question *Credis in remissionem* sq. which recurs so often, there are traces of the Baptismal formula in 406. 3, 508. 13, and in 192. 20, 281. 4, which contain the word *pompae*, used by Cyprian only in this connexion.

[3] On which Koffmane, p. 78, lays stress. But the double genitive required in *manus inpositio episcopi*, which constantly occurs, is almost unknown in Cyprian's writings. I have only noted 262. 11, 665. 3.

266 *The Style and Language of St. Cyprian.*

absent, for instance, from *Ep.* 63, which is entirely devoted to the subject. Its sense is concrete; communicants are said *eucharistiam accipere*, *Test.* 3. 94 *tit.*, 280. 20, &c., and conversely, 519. 4 *ab episcopo . . . eucharistia datur*; 280. 11 *eucharistiam ad cibum cottidie sumimus; euchari..tiam contingere, adtingere*, ib. 10, 19; cf. 407, 24. The word is used as a synonym for *potus sanctificatus* 255. 20. In 768. 19 is an obscurely expressed passage where *eucharistiam facere* stands for the usual *sa rificium celebrai e*, as also in *Sent.* 1. *Sanctum Domini* occurs 248. 5, 256. 7, 10; 217. 12 the pleonastic *caro Christi et sanctum Domini*. This may be an ellipse for *sanctum Domini corpus* 514. 12; *corpus Domini* occurs alone 665. 3, &c. Once also, as already mentioned in the note on *gratia* to the last section, *gratia salutaris* is used in relation to *sanctum Domini*, 256. 14 *quando gratia salutaris in cinerem sancto fugiente mutetur*, where *sancto* must either stand for *Christo* or be a neuter abstract [1]. The usual title for the Eucharistic, service is *sacrificium*, either alone as in 256. 9, 697. 23, or more often *s. diuinum* or *dominicum*. The elliptic *dominicum* occurs 384. 20, 714. 13, 14, the last instance being plural. *Hostia dominica* is opposed to *falsa sacrificia* 226. 9, and must be equivalent to *sacrificium*; cf. *uictima* for σφαγή in the O. L. of Is. 53. 7 [2]. *Sollemnia* is used for the Eucharistic service, 255. 14 *sollemnibus adimpletis*, and 649. 26; in the latter passage also *sollemnitas* [3]. In 713. 22 the whole service seems to be called *oblatio*. For the use of *sacramentum* in connexion with the Eucharist, see note to § 7. The most remarkable example is *sacramentum crucis* 431. 17. *Celebrare* is the most usual verb with *sacrificium*, *Test.* 1. 16. *tit.*, 256. 9, 466. 19, &c.; 830. 16

---

[1] *Fug.* 25 (25. 18 Reiff.) *ex ore, quo Amen in sanctum protuleris* seems to be the only similar case in Tertullian. Can it mean to say the response after the *Ter sanctus?*

[2] Ronsch, *Itala u. Vulgata*, p. 327, and Cyprian 80. 8, 414. 11, 507. 7. Perhaps also in 402. 21 *cum ad uictimam Christi confundantur sidera* is the true reading.

[3] Joh. 13. 1 in Tert. *Prax.* 23 has *sollemnitas Paschae* (Vulg. *dies festus*). *Sollemnia* and *sollemnitas* are constantly used by Tertullian of Christian and heathen rites.

facultas offerendi et celebrandi sacrificia diuina[1]. *Sacrificare* occurs 255. 10, but was no doubt avoided through its painful suggestion of the lapsed *sacrificati*. *Sanctificare calicem*, &c., e.g. 255. 21, 701. 17; *sacrificium dominicum legitima sanctificatione celebrare* 708. 10 Beside the use of *offerre sacrificia* already named, 736. 23, 830. 16, it is employed absolutely 479. 15 *offerre apud confessores*, and with *pro* of persons either dead or living (for the latter see § 26) 465. 19, 514. 12. 583. 11. *Oblationem facere pro dormitione* 467. 2 is equivalent to *sacrificium celebrare pro dormitione* 466. 19. *Offerre oblationes eorum* occurs 568. 14; *calix qui offertur*, sc. *Deo* 702. 9; *celebrare oblationes et sacrificia* 503. 21, cf. the use above mentioned of *oblatio* 713. 22. The Eucharist is a *commemoratio* both of Christ 702. 9, cf. 713. 13, and of the martyrs 503. 14, 504. 1, 583. 12. It will be seen that the name of a part of the Eucharistic service is often put for the whole; cf. especially 713. 21 *sic enim incipit et a passione Christi in persecutionibus fraternitas retardari dum in oblationibus discit de sanguine eius et cruore confundi*, i.e. from fear of being detected through the smell of wine[2].

Some of these terms are used of the worshippers as well as

---

[1] *Celebrare* is a favourite verb of Cyprian's. Besides this use of *celebrare sacrificia = sacrificare*, used also of heathen sacrifice, 673. 16, there are also *celebrare orationes = orare* 274. 7, 292. 4; *celebrare diuinas lectiones* 580. 24; *lauacra cottidie = lauari* 259. 6; *tot martyria iustorum saepe celebrata = perpetrata* 337. 8; *benedictionem celebrare circa Abraham = benedicere* 704. 7; (*patrimonium*) *unde opus caeleste celebratur*, i.e. charity, 380. 11; *acies adhuc geritur et agon cottidie celebratur* 526. 15, and similarly 389. 20 *quale munus est cuius editio celebratur = quod editur*; *sic spiritalibus meritis et caelestibus praemiis temporum uicissitudo celebratur* = the confessors pass their time, 578. 5. In this vague sense the word is very common in the more rhetorical parts of Cyprian's writings. Compare De Rebapt. 2 (A. 71. 21) *notissima omnibus praedicatio celebrata atque coepta a Iohanne Baptista*. *Celebrare resurrectionem Domini* occurs 292. 25, 714. 20 = commemorate, and so 583. 12, *martyrum dies anniuersaria commemoratione*, and 503. 15. In 193. 12 a passage of Scripture is introduced by *scriptum est ... et in exemplum nostri ecclesiae ore celebratur* = is proclaimed; 763. 13 *cuius aequalitatis sacramentum* (type) *uidemus in Exodo esse celebratum. Cogere et celebrare concilium* 775. 5.

[2] Cf. Hieron. Ep. 114. 2 *sacrosque calices et sancta uelamina et cetera quae ad cultum dominicae pertinent passionis*.

of the celebrant. *Sacrificium* in 384. 22 is used of their offering; they are called *sacrificantes* 255. 27, though this is rendered uncertain by comparison with l. 10; cf. 269. 2 *quando in unum cum fratribus conuenimus et sacrificia diuina cum Dei sacerdote celebramus.*

Altare is constant in Cyprian of the Christian altar. In 688. 2, 722. 4 he contrasts heathen *arae* with *Dei altare*; cf. 360. 4. Once a heathen altar is called *diaboli altare* 679. 23 (so Tert. *De Pallio* 4 *altaria bustuaria*), but he never speaks of *ara Dei*[1]; in his most violent attacks upon schism he always speaks of *altaria profana*, never of *arae*. *Nudor altarium*, of heathen worship, 24. 14, is one of many strong evidences that *Quod Id.* is not by Cyprian.

Communicatio[2], and sometimes the full form *ius communicationis* is common; *communicationem tribuere* 249. 9, *ius communicationis accipere* 518. 20, *laxare* 247. 28, &c. The verb *communicare* is equally common; *cum aliquo* 467. 18, 732 6, &c, being used of the recipient, *alicui* of the celebrant, 568. 13, 632. 9, &c. But there are a few exceptions, as 519. 21, 624. 8,

---

[1] Yet in the O. L. *ara* was certainly frequent, perhaps constant, in a good sense. In *Apoc.* 6. 9 Cyprian reads it three times, 130. 14, 250. 8, 413. 7. In this verse Tertullian has twice (*Res. Carn.* 25, *De An.* 9) turned it into *sub altari*, but he is paraphrasing the passage. Elsewhere he uses the words indifferently; cf. Kolberg, p. 212 f. Primasius retains *ara*. It occurs in this sense in *Claiom.* in Heb. 7. 13, and in *ff.* in Jac. 2. 21. In the Vulgate it is only found in the Apocryphal books, which were not revised by Jerome. Arnobius uses the words indifferently, and often in combination, of the heathen altar; Lactantius, I think, does the same. Ammianus, 22. 11. 9, uses *ara* of the Christian altar, perhaps in insult. In the Index to the first part of *C. I. L.* viii. (the African volume) *ara* occurs thirty-five times of the heathen altar, *altare* only once. The Christian altar is not named. The second part of *C. I. L.* viii. is unindexed, but in reading it through I did not notice anything inconsistent with the view that in ordinary language the words were thoroughly differentiated. In Virgil, *Ecl* 5. 65 *en quattuor aras, Ecce duas tibi, Daphni, duas altaria Phoebo*, the word *altare* seems more dignified than *ara*. It is certainly also rare in Augustan prose. Being stately and uncommon it was well adapted to the Christian need.

[2] *Communio* is rare, and only used in general senses, as 789 11 *nullam communionem lumini et tenebris* 758. 4, 10, &c. Cf. the curious use, 545. 15 *cum martyribus in honore communis est* = *particeps*. Yet in the Roman *Ep.* 8 (487. 20) *communio* = *communicatio*, and also in *Ep.* 75 (825. 18).

800. 2, where *communicare cum aliquo* is used of the celebrant. The verb is used absolutely, in the sense of *communicationem accipere* 588. 18, 740. 17; similarly *non communicantes* for *abstenti* 262. 1[1]. It may be mentioned here that the *Sursum corda* is entitled a *praefatio*, 289. 15.

§ 17. Prayer is usually *prex* or *oratio*. When the word stands alone, *prex*, not *preces*, is almost constant; in the compounds favoured by Cyprian *prex* seldom occurs. *Preces et orationes* in pleonasm is common, 272. 10, 465. 12, 578. 25, 596. 1 (twice), 688. 22; *prex et oratio* 267. 18, 276. 10; *petitiones et preces* 287. 6; *preces orationis* 500. 15; *postulationum preces* 319. 12. *Petitio* is fairly common; *precatio*, 268. 3, is rare. The most common verb is *rogare*; *orare* is also frequent, as is *petere*; *precari* and *postulare* (five times in *Dom. Or.*) not so common. *Deprecari* is used for *orare* 275. 3, 287. 10, 288. 15, 841. 16, as well as in its usual sense; cf. Thielmann in Wölfflin's *Archiv*, 1892, p. 253. Elaborate phrases, such as 501. 7 *oratione communi et concordi prece orantes*, are of course numerous. *Adorare, adorator* (e.g. 267. 20, from Joh. 4. 23) are confined to indirect citations from Scripture. The Lord's Prayer is *prex cottidiana*, as in Aug. *C. D.* 21. 27 (Dombart, ed. 2, ii. 548. 30).

For thanksgiving the language is not remarkable, except in the use of *uotum*, e.g. 504. 18 *quid enim uel maius in uotis meis potest esse uel melius quam cum uideo confessionis uestrae honore inluminatum gregem Christi?* i.e. 'for what can I be more thankful?' It is often practically equivalent to, and used with, *gaudium*; 728. 13 *uenientes... cum uoto et gaudio suscipio*, 614. 11 *uoti communis amplissimum gaudium excepimus*, 641. 11 (*filium*) *cum uoto paternae exultationis amplectitur*, 510. 22, 619. 12, &c.; so in other writers 557. 17, 620. 8, and Quint. 12. 5. 6 [2].

[1] In a badly worded phrase of Stephanus, cited 799. 18, 814. 8, he seems to use *communicare aliquem* for *alicui*. Cyprian takes evident pleasure in pointing out that his opponent's diction is on a level with his arguments; *quae inperite atque inprouide scripsit* 799. 14.

[2] *Votum* is also often used in the classical sense of desire, e.g. 308. 23

There is not much that is noteworthy concerning watching, literal or metaphorical, and fasting. *In frequentanda oratione nocte uigilare* 288. 22, *inuigilare et incumbere ad preces* 289. 11, *uigilare in satisfactione Dei* 522. 17, and the like are frequent. *Ieiunium*, 377. 13, &c. is common.

§ 18. *Ecclesia*, as the body of Christians,—*ecclesia id est plebs in ecclesia constituta* 711. 18—has already been considered. In *Test.* 3. 46 tit. *mulierem in ecclesia tacere debere* he is borrowing Scriptural language; but 508. 20 *ad ecclesiam reuerti* may mean the place of assembly. This is more probable in 686. 3, where Cyprian speaks of Felicissimus and his companions as not having the courage *ad ecclesiae limen accedere*. But there are no instances so clear as some in Tertullian of this sense of the word. *Statio* is used 598. 9, and also by Cornelius, 612. 7. The only furniture of the Church mentioned beside the altar is the *pulpitum*, from which the lector read the Scripture. The *pulpitum* in 583. 24 is *tribunal ecclesiae*, and the lector *loci altioris celsitate subnixus*. In 581. 1 the exchange by the confessor Aurelius of the *catasta* for the *pulpitum*, on his ordination to the lectorship, gains the more in point the greater the resemblance between the two. In *Pass. Perp.* 19 Saturninus is exposed upon a *pulpitum* at his martyrdom. In *Pass. Perp.* 5, 6 the prisoners' station in court is *catasta*, rendered in the Greek by βῆμα. Rutilius Namatianus (1. 393) in the fifth century describes Christian sermons as *mendacis deliramenta catastae*. Thus it had come to be equivalent to pulpit. The two words must have been identical in meaning; a platform affording a full view of the person reading, on sale (Pers. 6. 77, &c.), or under trial or torture.

It is remarkable that Cyprian seems to avoid giving a definite name to the Christian meeting. He is contented with vague language, like *colligi* 222. 4 (cf. 659. 15; never the vulgar *colligere* of Tertullian and others; Koffmane, p. 47,

maiora desideria et uota potiora, 351. 15 *studio magis contradicendi quam uoto discendi*, 510. 1, 656. 7, 686. 17, &c.

The Language of St. Cyprian. 271

Rönsch, *It. V.* p. 353), where, however, *extra ecclesiam* may be local; *in unum conuenire* 269. 1. Perhaps, indeed, there was no permanent church in Carthage. A comparison of 600. 22 *considentibus Dei sacerdotibus et altari posito* at a Council, with 688. 1 *recedentibus sacerdotibus ac Domini altare remouentibus*, suggests that the place of meeting was not permanently devoted to its purpose. Had there been a church the Council would no doubt have met there. But the *cleri nostri sacer uenerandusque congestus* of the latter passage was in all probability a dais, and must have been cumbrous for removal. There is no such use of the word in Georges' Dictionary, and it may possibly, as already suggested, be equivalent to *consessus*, but cf. Apul. *De Deo Socr.* 4 (p. 9. 14 Goldbacher), *usque ad regni nutabilem suggestum et pendulum tribunal euectus*. And when in 688. 1 we read *ut ecclesia Capitolio cedat* it seems as though each were a building, and each perhaps single of its kind.

§ 19. Beside the acts of worship already mentioned there remains the sermon of the bishop. No one else is named by Cyprian as addressing the people. In 527. 20 he speaks of *allocutio et persuasio*. This was by letter, but Cyprian's letters addressed to the people were really speeches, some of them of the most rhetorical character, written to be delivered for him in the assembly. Though *allocutio* was a recognized term (Tert., Novatian in *Ep.* 30 and later writers; see Matzinger on *De Bono Pud.* p. 14) Cyprian never uses it again. Instead he constantly uses *tractatus*; *tractatio* never. *Tractare*, in the sense of preaching, occurs in the Preface to the *Testimonia*, 36. 3, where Cyprian states that his object in writing is *non tam tractasse quam tractantibus materiam praebuisse*. He repeats this, as he usually does with what seem to him happy phrases, in the Preface to the *Ad Fortunatum*, 318. 11 *ut non tam tractatum meum uidear tibi misisse quam materiam tractantibus praebuisse*. As *tractantes* in the second clause of both certainly means preachers, the word must have the same meaning in the first. The verb recurs in the same sense 633. 17, 659. 15, 842. 1, the noun 219. 3, 383. 7, and in

Ep. 77 by Nemesianus, 834. 7 *non desinis in tractatibus tuis sacramenta occulta nudare*[1].

§ 20. There is not much variety in the mode of address by the clergy to one another and to the laity. *Frater* is normal in both cases, the laity are *fratres et sorores* 473. 8, cf. the common *fraternitas*; *lector frater noster* 565. 14. In directly addressing his correspondents the word rarely stands alone; in the hostile *Ep.* 66 to Florentius always, and also often in the fiiendly *Ep.* 59 to Cornelius. Elsewhere in that letter the usual *frater carissime* is used. A bishop is called *filius* in 469. 4, and Quirinus of the *Testimonia*, addressed as *fili carissime*, may have been a bishop also, and certainly belonged to the clergy, as the *Magnus filius* of *Ep.* 74, and others so styled by Cyprian may also have done. The only epithets used, except the neutral *desiderantissimus* of the final salutations, are *carissimus* and *dilectissimus*. Of these the former is used for the most part in addressing clergy, the latter in addressing laity, though there are sundry exceptions[2]. *Dilectissimus* is constantly employed in *Ep.* 58, to the *plebs* of Thibaris, in which the Bishop and Clergy of that place, who must have been at variance with Cyprian, are ignored. It is also usual in the treatises, e.g. *de Un.*, *B. Pat.*, *Dom. Or.* *Carissimus* is used more irregularly. Its common use is to the clergy, clergy jointly with laity, or the confessors. Yet in *Ep.* 43, addressed to the *plebs* only, they are *carissimi* four times, *dilectissimi* thrice. But bishops also are called *dilectissimi*, e.g. 435. 11, 806. 15, and in *Ep.* 67, addressed to clergy

---

[1] From *De Bono Pud.* I (A. 13. 5) *cotidianis euangeliorum tractatibus* the sermon seems to have been part of the daily Eucharistic service, cf. ib. 14. 1. Matzinger, *Des hl Cypr. Tractat de B. Pud.*, Nurnberg, 1892, has shown strong grounds for regarding this treatise as Cyprian's; cf. p. 194. Cyprian uses the noun twice (623. 14, 632. 3), the verb four times (510. 3, 545. 7, 565. 19, 570. 7) of proceedings in Council, where the speeches no doubt had some resemblance to sermons. *Tractatus* appears to be used several times in the *De Rebapt.* in the sense of argument. *Praeconium* (add to Hartel's list 237. 14, 363. 9) is never used in this sense by Cyprian, as Koffmane, p. 97, asserts.

[2] See Wolfflin's most instructive article in his *Archiv*, 1892, p. 19. Nothing can be learned from the recent papers of Babl and Engelbrecht on this subject.

The Language of St. Cyprian. 273

as well as laity, *dilectissimus* is constant, except in the final salutation, where *carissimi* stands; but the genuineness of this salutation is doubtful.

Dominus is never used by Cyprian. He is so addressed by other bishops, 836. 3, and the word is used several times in the *Epp.* by persons of different classes to their equals and superiors, much as it is in Apul. *Metam. Papa, Papas* is confined to Novatian and other Roman writers in their addresses to Cyprian. Cornelius never uses it. *Benedictus* (used in the Rom. *Ep.* 8, 485. 19, *Pass. Perp.* 3, Tert. *Prae cr.* 30, &c.) is never used by Cyprian either of the living or of the dead. *Beatus* is constantly used for confessors and martyrs; *beatissimus* more rarely, both of the living and dead, e. g. 492. 15, 828. 13.

In addressing others Cyprian often speaks modestly of *mediocritas nostra* (101. 15, 297. 11, 317. 8, 435. 12, 527. 15, 22, 576. 18, 623. 20, 749. 5, 760. 19, 799. 1; *parua nostra mediocritas* 765. 22), for *ego*, an expression apparently first used by Velleius, 2, 111. 3. Elsewhere he uses the word as an abstract in similar passages; e. g. 4. 7, 568. 6, 656. 10, 702. 1, 798. 9. Other examples of self-depreciation are 189. 19 *extremi et minimi et humilitatis nostrae admodum conscii*, 309. 16 *minimus et extremus*, 500. 8 *minimus famulus*. The two last are justified by being used of himself as favoured with a vision. There is no formal system of abstraction, *sanctitas tua*, &c. in Cyprian (cf. Wölfflin in his *Archiv*, 1892, p. 3), yet there is a certain approximation to it; e. g. 495. 13 *admoneo religiosam sollicitudinem uestram*, 588. 3 *diligentia uestra*, 504. 15, 676. 13, 775. 7, &c.

It is worthy of notice that Christians in Cyprian's *Epp.* invariably have only one name, in spite of the obvious inconvenience of this in a country so ill-provided as Africa. The only exceptions are in *Ep.* 66, where Cyprian follows the example of his opponent Puppianus in giving himself two names, coupled, in the manner usual in the African inscriptions, by *qui et*[1], and the two Geminii of *Ep.* 1. The same is

[1] E. g. in the unindexed supplement to *C. I. L.* 8, 12499, 14513, 14936,

274 *The Style and Language of St. Cyprian.*

the case in the very numerous monumental inscriptions found in the ruins of the great church of Carthage.

§ 21. The payment of the clergy by the laity is rarely mentioned by Cyprian. In 724. 4 he mentions *stipes, oblationes, lucra*; the second is used again, 838. 12, in a passage which shows that it does not necessarily mean Eucharistic oblations. In three other passages he gives what are evidently definite technical terms; 466. 12 *in honore sportulantium fratrum tamquam decimas ex fructibus accipientes ab altari et sacrificiis non recedant*, 571. 1 *interea se a diuisione mensurna tantum contineant*, 585. 1 *ut et sportulis idem cum presbyteris honorentur et diuisiones mensurnas aequatis quantitatibus partiantur.* There are thus three sources of income : (1) the *stips*, which is the *stips menstrua* of the Church in its organization as a guild, and forms the *diuisio mensurna* [1]. This must also be the *stipendia ecclesiae episcopo dispensante* of 588. 14. (2) *Oblationes*, which can only have been an irregular source of income. (3) *Sportula* and *honor*, with *sportulare* and *honorare*. *Honor, honorare* must have a definite sense, like the *honor medici* [2], and *sportula* must have the same sense as in the guilds, where periodical distributions were made to the members from the interest of legacies, gifts of the rich, or a general subscription ; cf. Schiess *op. cit.* p. 103. The *sportulae* differed in amount according to the rank of the members in the society ; cf. Tert. *Ieiun.* 17 (297. 2 Reiff.). Thus in 585. 1 the ordained confessors are to have the same *sportula* as the presbyters ; i. e. probably less than the deacons received. Cyprian says nothing about the days chosen instead of the heathen festivals, imperial birthdays, &c., on which the *sportulae* were distributed in ordinary guilds. It is curious,

16608, and once (cf. Hoffmann, *Index Grammaticus ad Africae titulos*, p. 112) *Caecilia Festiua qui et Leda*, 16919.

[1] Cf. Schiess, *Die röm. Collegia Funeraticia*, p. 75. The contributions must have been heavy, since they had to provide stipends, as well as to meet the usual expenses of a burial club.

[2] Perhaps *Relatio Symmachi*, § 15 *cum religionum ministros honor publicus pasceret* has the same meaning. Symmachus is pleading against the abolition of the endowments of the temples.

though probably nothing more, that under the Empire there should have grown up a system of *sportulae* for the maintenance of the Roman worship : cf. Mommsen, *Staatsrecht*, ii. 63.

§ 22. Of Christian virtues the one most commonly inculcated is *disciplina*. Of *disciplina* one sense, in which it represents διδασκαλία, has already been mentioned in § 6. It stands more often for loyalty or obedience to the law of God, and of conduct resulting from such obedience, e. g. 268. 18 *precatio cum disciplina quietem continens et pudorem*, where *cum disciplina* is adverbial, 269. 3 *uerecundiae et disciplinae memores*, both of the conduct of worshippers; 429. 15 *ad patrem Deum deifica disciplina respondeat*, 618. 22 *nec remanere in ecclesia Dei possunt qui deificam et ecclesiasticam disciplinam nec actus sui conuersatione nec morum pace tenuerunt*[1]; 584. 16, *ut magisterium caeteris praebeat disciplinae*, 742. 21, 527. 7[2], &c. It is not always easy to distinguish cases in which the thought is that of military discipline from those in which it is of religious teaching. Practically identical with *disciplina*, in its sense of 'loyal obedience,' are sometimes *censura* (see note to § 3) and often *uigor*, though it is more often used of the bishop in his capacity of judge than of other Christians, loyal under pressure[3]. *Integer, integritas*, also in the sense of 'loyalty,' are common.

[1] In these two passages *deifica disciplina* is simply equivalent to *disciplina dominica* 505. 21. See § 1.

[2] *Disciplina* is often used with, or in the same sense as, *censura*, e. g. 666. 12 *litteras ... et ecclesiasticae disciplinae et sacerdotalis censurae plenas*, 625. 14, &c. In 592. 24 *disciplina* is contrasted with *misericordia*. Closely connected with its use of the teaching of Scripture is that of *disciplina euangelica*, the law of the Gospel, 592. 19, 709. 23, 713. 18, &c. It stands for a lesson learnt, 303. 16 *hanc apostoli disciplinam de Domini lege tenuerunt non mussitare in aduersis*, 802. 12; of proficiency in what has been taught, 9. 5 *disciplina est ut perimere quis possit*. The contrast between the *disciplina* of public and the *conuersatio* of private life, which Kolberg (p. 164 n.) traces in Tertullian, cannot be established for Cyprian In other respects the two use the word in the same senses and with equal frequency.

[3] *Vigor* has a wide and vague use. It is most common as equivalent to *censura*, in the sense named above; 199. 17, 730. 20, &c. *Censura uigoris* 744. 16, and *censurae uigor* 284. 14, are identical pleonastic terms. It is also used for 'severity,' 326. 4, 608. 11, &c.; cf. in the Roman *Ep.* 36 *uigor tuus et*

276 The Style and Language of St. Cyprian.

Caritas and *dilectio* (once, in *Test.* 3. 3 *tit. agape et dilectio*) are equally common. *Adfectio* seems only once (232. 1) to be used of the virtue; elsewhere it is of personal feeling. *Concordia* (*concordia pacis* 217. 23, 220. 17 and *concordiae pax* 285. 11). *Pax* (*pax morum* 618. 23, cf. 621. 17; the adjectives corresponding to it are *pacatus* once, 221. 5 *simplices et pacati*, *pacificus* constantly[1]), *quies*, *uerecundia*, *continentia* in the patristic sense, and *humilitas*[2] are constantly mentioned. The right feeling of man towards God is usually *timor*, e.g. 526. 7 (*timere* 302. 27, and often, *timidus* 501. 10, *timide ac religiose* 716. 7), more rarely *metus* 392. 26, &c., with *metuere* 737. 21, &c. *Trementes ac metuentes Deum* occurs 567. 10; *humilem et quietum et trementem sermones suos* 506. 2. *Obsequium* and *obseruatio* are very common, 392. 29, 741. 23, &c. *Deuotio* is not very common; 631. 5 *deuotio et timor*; 660. 9 *deuotionis fides* equivalent to *fidelis deuotio* 786. 10; *deuote et fortiter* 513. 9, *deuota uirtus* 663. 23, &c., *fidelissimus ac deuotissimus frater* 503. 16. The meaning is always that of loyalty. *Dicatus Deo* (see Hartel's *Index*), according to Bünemann on Lact. *Epit.* 71. 8, first occurs in Cyprian. *Iustus* is fairly common as equivalent to 'righteous,' e.g. 681. 4 *confessores et uirgines et iustos quosque fidei laude praecipuos*; so also *iustitia*, 431. 7, includes all the virtues previously

---

... *seueritas* (572. 18), and 551. 16, also Roman. It means also the right to jurisdiction, 469. 13 *pro episcopatus uigore et cathedrae auctoritate*, 667. 14, &c. In all these cases it is exactly equal to *disciplina*. It is also often used quite classically for 'power' or 'energy'; 6. 18, 361. 6, 725. 10, &c. *Vigor fidei* is very common, 339. 25, 630. 24, &c.; *uigor continentiae* 638. 16. *Vigor*, *disciplina*, *censura*, *robur*, *tenor* (*tenorem tenere* 621. 17, 725. 9, *tenore custoditae fidei uigere* 828. 17, *si tenor fidei praeualet apud uos* 806. 15, &c.) are all used separately and in combination without any definite difference of meaning.

[1] *Pax* is also frequently contrasted with *turbo*, *tempestas*, *procella* of persecution or heresy.

[2] *Humilis*, *humilitas* are almost always used in the Christian sense; cf. 507. 16 *humiles et quieti et taciturni* (unmurmuring), and in the Roman *Ep.* 31 (563. 1) *humilitas et subiectio*. In 730. 24 the *humilitas* of brigands to their chief; in 189. 19, 689. 4 it means 'lowly position.' *Humiliare* (373. 7) is rare, except in Scriptural reminiscences.

The Language of St. Cyprian. 277

mentioned. Similar uses are 7. 1, 223. 20, 623. 10[1]. *Fides*, as the Christian Faith and in relation to Baptism, has been already mentioned. As a virtue of the individual Christian it is also used in the Scriptural way: e.g. 672. 17 *fides qua uiuimus*. There seems to be nothing peculiar about the manner of its employment. The uses of *credere* are sufficiently given in Hartel's *Index*[2].

§ 23. Charity and alms are often described as *eleemosynae*. The singular perhaps only occurs in *Test.* 3. 1 (111. 12) *nemini negandam eleemosynam* and 377. 10. The plural seems always to mean 'acts of mercy,' *eleemosynas facere* being the most common use 379. 23, &c., from Acts 10. 2, &c.; cf. 290. 21; there is nothing like *eleemosynas dare*. *Misericordia*, according to Koffmane, p. 30, was first introduced by Cyprian as a translation of *eleemosyna*[3]. In *Test.* 3. 1 *tit. de bono operis et misericordiae* becomes in § 2 *tit. in opere et eleemosynis*. These are, as is usual in Cyprian, simple pleonasms. *Misericordia* is very common in *Op. El.*, e.g. 374. 22 *addidit eleemosynas esse faciendas; misericors monet misericordiam fieri*, which are identical phrases; 375. 18 *misericordiae opera*; 376. 17 *operationibus iustis Deo satisfieri, misericordiae meritis peccata purgari*, and many more. *Miserationes pauperum* = 'acts of mercy to the poor,' occurs 379. 24, from Dan. 4. 24 (377. 6). But the common word for acts of charity is *operatio*, often with the epithet *iusta* (see note to the last §) as in 374. 9, 384. 11, but also without, 382. 27, 503. 18, &c.[4] *Opus* in the

[1] The word is often also used in the sense of 'adequate'; *paenitentia plena et iusta* 636. 14, *datur opera ne satisfactionibus et lamentationibus iustis delicta redimantur* 680. 21, &c. It is difficult to see the exact meaning in 651. 18 *obtemperandum est ostensionibus adque admonitionibus iustis*; in the Roman *Ep.* 31 (561. 22) *de tuis laboribus iustis* is from the LXX of Prov. 3. 9. For *iustitia* as a rendering of the Biblical δικαιοσύνη in the sense of 'alms' see the next section, and J. B. Mayor's valuable note on Jac. 5. 20 on the theological use of δικαιοσύνη.

[2] For *credere Christo*, &c. add 362. 26, 404. 2, 422. 18, 596. 10, 729. 16; for *credere aliquem*, *Sent.* 14 and A. 72. 11; *credere contra aliquem* 734. 10.

[3] Yet Tert. *Adu. Marc.* 4 37 has *misericordiae opera*, and cf. *Fug.* 13 *in*.

[4] In other senses the word is rare; 7. 1 *operatio iusta* seems used generally of a righteous life; 466. 8 *Leuitica tribus ... qui operationibus diuinis insistebant*.

278 The Style and Language of St. Cyprian.

singular is not very common in this sense, *Test.* 3. 1, 2, 26 *tit.*, 385. 10, &c., though the plural constantly occurs. *Opera* singular is absent, and the plural *operae* is only used by the illiterate Celerinus, 531. 4. *Operari* is also common, e. g. *Test.* 3. 40 *tit. non iactanter nec tumultuose operandum.* *Operans* occurs as an adjective 394. 3, and 407. 1 *iusti et operantes*, and also *operarius* 379. 17, *o. et fructuosus* 380. 3[1]. The last, with its contrary *sterilis*, is often used. *Iustitia* is often used for 'charity.' The word is no doubt derived from δικαιοσύνη, regarded as an exact equivalent for ἐλεημοσύνη, in such Biblical passages as Matt. 6. 1. There is no rendering of this verse in Cyprian, but the Vulgate has *iustitiam*, and probably Cyprian had the same, though *k* reads *elemosinam*. At any rate there are many other Biblical passages from which he might have borrowed the word; cf. Meyer's *Commentary* on *Matt.* 6. 1. The word is thoroughly adopted and used freely and naturally by Cyprian; *iustitiae opera* 314. 5, *iustitiae ac misericordiae nostrae opera* 392. 19, and *iusta operatio* often in *Op. El.*; *iusti et operantes*, synonymous, 407. 1; cf. 307. 5. As has been already stated, *pius, pietas* are not used by Cyprian in this sense. 'To distribute alms' is commonly *dispensare* 393. 12, 588. 14, 700. 19, &c.[2]

§ 24. The distinctively Christian *conuersatio*, for 'manner of life,' is not much more common than *actus*. Their strict meanings seem to be reversed in 739. 13 *episcopus deligatur plebe praesente quae . . . uniuscuiusque actum de eius conuersatione perspexit*, where *actus* must mean 'character' and *conuersatio* 'conduct.' Elsewhere the words seem to be used

---

[1] *Opus, operari* occur in several senses; *opera saecularia, funesta* 633. 6, 636. 3, &c. In 837. 20 Nemesianus strangely writes *sacrificium ex omni opere mundo*. *Operari in aliquem* = 'to relieve,' 386. 8, 'to injure,' 483. 8; *operari ad bonos usus, necessitates*, &c., 195. 23, 479. 4, 700. 28; *circa fructum salutis operantes* = 'to win,' 390. 2; *magis ac magis intellectus cordis operabitur scrutanti scripturas* 36. 18; *operatur per inprobas mentes uirus* 12. 3; *clauo funibus uelis ut fabricetur et armetur nauis operare* 647. 1. The verb is transitive in 11. 6.

[2] *Expungere* in the very hastily written *Ep.* 41 (587. 13, 588. 5) cannot be regarded as an ecclesiastical term.

The Language of St. Cyprian. 279

indifferently. *Conuersari* is very rare in this sense; e. g. 274. 13 and in *Ep.* 75 (817. 21).

Religio has a wide use, though such phrases as *religio christiana* do not occur[1]. It is often employed of the religious frame of mind as in 204. 19 *iustitiam cum religione retinentes, stabiles in fide* sq., which, in Cyprian's language, is probably equivalent to *religiose,* 303. 2 *circa timorem Dei stabilis et firmus et ad omnem tolerantiam passionis fide religionis armatus,* 742. 9 *permanet apud plurimos sincera mens et religio integra,* 743. 17 f. *integritatis et fidei uestrae religiosam sollicitudinem laudamus et adhortamur ne . . . sed integram et sinceram fidei uestrae firmitatem religioso timore seruetis,* Test. 3. 3 tit. *agapem et dilectionem religiose et firmiter exercendam* 193. 28, 250. 17, &c. It will be seen that the word is used in passages where there is the notion of steadiness and of awe. The preceding passages have referred to the laity only or to all Christians; but the word is also specially used of the debates and decisions of Bishops and Councils, as 466. 16 *episcopi antecessores nostri religiose considerantes et salubriter providentes,* 716. 7 *sollicite et timide ac religiose,* ib. 25 *religioni nostrae congruit et timori et ipsi loco adque officio sacerdotii nostri,* 736. 20, 805. 9, &c. The connotation of *inreligiosus* is the same, 415. 12 *inreligiosa et inuerecunda festinatio,* 741. 12 *nec nos moueat . . . si apud quosdam aut lubrica fides nutat aut Dei timor inreligiosus uacillat*[2].

---

[1] Yet cf. 741. 25 *Iudaeis deficientibus et a religione diuina recedentibus,* 369. 24 *uerae religionis candida lux* contrasted with *tenebrosa superstitio.*

[2] Beside this general use of *religio* it appears to have definitely that of 'Orders' in two passages; 586. 10 *et promouebitur quidem (Numidicus presbyter) ad ampliorem gradum religionis suae,* i. e. *sacerdotium,* 629. 11 (*Cornelius*) *per omnia ecclesiastica officia promotus . . . ad sacerdotii sublime fastigium cunctis religionis gradibus ascendit.* So also 510. 15 *administratio religiosa* stands for the usual *ecclesiastica.* But in 478. 14, though a similar passage, *religio* has quite a general sense, as also probably in 600. 22 *in tanto fratrum religiosoque conuentu,* i. e. *tam religioso* (cf. 609. 2 *tanta laetitia adfecti sumus et Deo . . . gratias agimus,* sc. *tantas.* Such omissions of a particle through the same preceding are common in Cyprian; see p 198 n.). The word comes to mean rule, 465. 18 *cuius ordinationis et religionis formam Leuitae prius in lege tenuerunt,* where there are three synonyms; in 686. 18,

280 *The Style and Language of St. Cyprian.*

Christians are thrice described as *fundati super petram* 210. 16, 579. 9, 625. 4; cf. 188. 10. *Christus qui est petra* occurs 706. 19[1]. Progress in Christian life is expressed by *proficere*, which is constantly used in all possible constructions[2]. The result is *promereri Deum*, used by Cyprian at least twenty-three times[3]; *merita* means almost as often 'punishment' as 'reward,' 359. 8, 496. 19, &c. The metaphor of *agon, palma,* &c. is used of a good life as well as of confessorship, 394. 21 ff., and elsewhere.

§ 25. Sin[4] is *peccatum* or *delictum*, the former being the more usual. *Peccator*, both as a substantive and as an attribute (*sacerdos sacrilegus et peccator* 769. 2, &c.), is common; *delictor* only occurs 720. 17. *Delinquere*[5] is somewhat 713. 18 it seems equivalent to *disciplina* and *censura*. In one passage, 698. 20 f., it seems used of a bond, according to the old etymology; *et non tantum dilectio sed et religio instigare nos debeat ad fratrum corpora redimenda.* Here *religio* refers to the *adunatio, dilectio* to *fratres* preceding. There remain the three passages 467. 4 *sacerdotum decretum religiose et necessarie factum*, 605. 13 *et religiosum uobis et necessarium existimaui ... ad confessores litteras facere*, 701. 19 *religiosum pariter ac necessarium duxi de hoc ad uos litteras facere*. The third of these shows that in the second *uobis* cannot be construed with *litteras facere*; and Cyprian never has *litteras facere alicui*. *Vobis* must be equivalent to *erga uos* and *religiosum, religiose* taken in a general sense in all three cases.

[1] The word *petra* is used literally once, 667. 24.

[2] Hartel's list of these constructions is by no means complete. The word is very sparingly used by Tertullian; it is constantly used by Seneca of moral progress, and very possibly is a part of Cyprian's debt to him.

[3] To Hartel's instances add 392. 28, 483. 11, 494. 19, 511. 5, 525. 11, 539. 7, 629. 10, 831. 8, *Vita*, c. 3. All have *Deum* or *Dominum* as direct object, except 494. 19 *coronam de eo promerendam*. The word is not used by the other writers in Cyprian's *Epp*, and rarely by Tertullian. It is used twice at least by Seneca instead of his usual *demereri*; *Dial.* 7. 24. 1, *Ben.* 2. 2. 1. Apuleius uses it thrice in *Met.* 5. 25, 6. 10, 11 6 (93. 23, 103. 8, 209. 6 Eyss.). The first and third have *Cupidinem, numen* as objects. The word did not hold its own in later theological literature; Ambr. *Ep.* 63. 112, Hier. *Ep.* 120. 10. Aug. *C. D.* 19. 16, 21. 27 are, I think, the only instances in those writings.

[4] Much of the language dealt with in this section, though generally applicable, is used by Cyprian only in relation to heresy or lapse, because he rarely has occasion to mention other sins. For the sake of convenience I have dealt with the whole here, instead of placing part in the later sections which deal with those subjects.

[5] *Delinquere magna* 262. 18 (cf. *peccare grauia* 228. 1), *delinquere in Deum* 717. 10, *delinquentes = delictores* 743. 4.

rare; *peccare* occurs on almost every page. *Mortale crimen* only occurs once, 407. 21[1], *mortalia docere* 469. 3, i. e. the art of acting. Heresy is *falsa et mortalis seductio* 725. 16, and lapse *summum delictum* 518. 2. *Vulnus*, especially in *Op. El.*, is very common for 'sin'[2]. The metaphor is carried out with great consistency; *uulnerati, sauciati, medella, cicatricem obducere, mortuus*, &c. are frequent; cf. 635. 17 ff. Almost as common is the metaphor of disease, *morbus, morbidus* (always, I think, active, as it is in Lucretius' description of the plague, 6. 957, &c.), *contagium*, &c. The Biblical *transgredi* and *transgressio*[3] do not occur in the plain sense of 'sin.' The only other common metaphor is that of *labes* 428. 10, &c., *sordes* 374. 17, &c. (singular, *Test*. 3. 54 *tit.*). There is nothing noteworthy about the names of particular sins; *zelus* with *zelare* (in *Z. L.* and elsewhere, as 693. 24) is common; *moechus* 638. 11, &c., is rare.

The duty of man in relation to sin is *paenitere*[4], or *paenitentiam agere*. *Plangere delicta* 261. 10, &c. (also intransitive 641. 17, 649. 12), and many similar words are used in this connexion. It may be said that much of the language which is used of Baptism as taking away sin, and most of that which is used of Christ's work, is repeated of human effort; cf. such passages as 375. 2, 646. 12. The result of righteousness is *redimere delicta* 195. 24, 387. 16, &c., *tergere peccata* once, 387. 25, *propitiari Deum* 376. 16 (cf. 366. 1), *placare Dominum* 249. 25. *Deponere* (641. 8, &c.), and *exponere* (e. g. 423. 26) *peccata* are used occasionally. Beside *paenitentia* the normal language concerning penitents includes *deprecatio, satisfactio* and *exhomologesis*; 227. 10 *in paenitentia criminis*

---

[1] *Adulterium, fraus, homicidium* are the crimes so defined. Cp. p. 299 n., and Harnack, *De Aleatt*. pp. 27, 84 ff.

[2] Cf. Miodoński's note to *De Aleatt*. p. 83.

[3] *Vulnera transgressionis* is used by Novatian 551. 21; *transgressio praecepti* occurs 409. 17, *loci sui ministerium transgressi* 757. 2, *transgressor legis* 404. 27. These are the only instances of the word in relation to sin: it never has the absolute meaning of *peccatum*, &c.

[4] As a personal verb it occurs 526. 16, 647. 13, the first followed by a genitive, the second alone.

282 The Style and Language of St. Cyprian.

constituti Deum plenis satisfactionibus deprecantur. Deprecatio, singular and plural, is common, 377. 14, &c., *satisfactio, satisfactiones, satisfacere, satisfieri* constantly occur; 247. 9, 472. 14, 516. 11, 522. 17, 680. 18, &c. *Exhomologesis* is the regular word for 'confession'; it occurs in the plural 524. 5[1]. *Confessio* is only used twice in this sense; 258. 18 where it is explained by *confiteantur* preceding, and 615. 13 in the sense of return from schism[2]. *Exhomologesin facere* is not so common as *confiteri*, or *confiteri peccata*. Cyprian's favourite metaphor for such penitent conduct is *pulsare ad ecclesiam* 682. 18, &c.[3] The reward of penitence and confession is *manus inpositio* 514. 11, &c. It is strange, however, though in all probability an accident, that the substantive is never used in this connexion; there is always a periphrasis; *manu eis a uobis in paenitentiam inposita* 525. 18, and the like. *Remissa*, &c. have already been treated of under the head of Baptism. *Absolutio* and its cognates (cf. Tert. *Adu. Marc.* 1. 28) are entirely absent.

The punishment of the impenitents (*contumaces* 248. 16, &c. is common, but hardly precise) is *abstineri*; *abstinere* transitive occurs, 475. 20, &c., ten times in all, *abstentus* also frequently[4]. The full form *abstinere a communicatione*, 590. 4, is not often used. *Cohibere a communicatione*, 597. 15, and *prohibere*, 280. 13, do not recur. The opposite to *abstinere* is *admittere* 636. 7, &c., or *pacem dare, concedere*, &c., e. g. 717. 15.

---

[1] The evidence is strongly in favour of *exhomologesis* instead of Hartel's *exhomologesin*; cf. the plural *haeresis* 781. 16, 800. 1, &c, which is the true reading, not *haereses*.

[2] Probably also 647. 12, though there it may have its usual sense. It was very natural that Cyprian should avoid it, since he has so much occasion to speak of confession in the other sense. But it is almost as rare in Tertullian; perhaps only *Adu. Marc.* ii. 24 *paenitentiae confessio, Apol.* 24, *Paen.* 3, 8, *Carn. Xti* 8.

[3] It is impossible to reconstruct from Cyprian the ceremony of penitence and readmission. But from *Ep.* 59. 15 it is clear that the account given by Tertullian in *Pud.* 13, though hostile, is not inaccurate. Tertullian's language in relation to sin, penitence, &c., is much the same as Cyprian's.

[4] For the construction of *abstinere* see Weinhold in Wolfflin's *Archiv*, 6. 509 ff.

The Language of St. Cyprian. 283

§ 26. Human responsibility is recognized as *arbitrium liberum*[1]; *Test.* 3. 52 *tit.*, 204. 1, 218. 16, 674. 15; cf. the common saving clause concerning bishops, e. g. 778. 5 *quando habeat in ecclesiae administratione uoluntatis suae arbitrium liberum unusquisque praepositus.* Man's mind and conscience is usually *conscientia*; the word has a wide extension of meaning[2].

§ 27. Human life is transitory (for *consistens* implying this see p. 311), and its end a summons or departure. *Mors, mori* are therefore usually paraphrased, and not often used of Christians without some qualification.

There is a great variety of language concerning death. *Arcessire, arcessitio,* from the Old Latin of such passages as Joh. 14. 3 (v. Rönsch, *It. V.* 284, and Wölfflin in his *Archiv,* 1893, p. 286), occur respectively twice and five times[3]. The

---

[1] So in Tertullian, *Adu. Marc.* ii. 5 *liberum et sui arbitrii et suae potestatis inuenio hominem a Deo institutum,* and elsewhere.

[2] In the sense of 'mind,' e.g. 832. 24 *conscientiae uictricis uigor,* 494. 14 *uoluntas integra et conscientia gloriosa,* 258. 12 *hoc eo proficit ut sit minor culpa, non ut innocens conscientia,* 253. 13, 387. 17, &c. So also *conscientia* is often contrasted with *manus,* mental action with bodily; 256. 24 *manus contaminare, conscientiam miscere,* 634. 5 *manus pura, conscientia polluta,* 528. 2, &c. *Ne quid conscientiam nostram lateret* 547. 12, and similar phrases are very common; 500. 17, 777. 24, &c. Hence the word comes to have the exact meaning of 'knowledge'; 346. 8 (*Paulus*) *qui id quod et didicit et uidit maioris conscientiae ueritate profitetur,* i. e. truth gained by fuller knowledge; of knowledge involving consent, 717. 14 *sine petitu et conscientia plebis,* 727. 4 *sine conscientia et permissu Dei,* cf. 738. 13, &c. This knowledge may be that possessed by others of a person's character; 619. 8 *hanc conscientiam criminum iam pridem timebat,* i. e. public knowledge; so 398. 20 *uirtutum conscientia* is contrasted with *iactantia*; the good character of Christians is well known, though they do not parade it as do the philosophers; so also 10. 26 and probably 631. 11 *qui conscientiae suae luce clarescunt. Conscientia sua* seems to mean the general knowledge of Cornelius' merit, not his own conscious innocence. The word also means the sense of innocence or of guilt, more often the latter than the former; so 11. 4, 591. 14, 618. 21, 727. 22. In 634. 10 *tolerabilis conscientia* = a not unbearable sense of sin. Hence the meaning of actual innocence or guilt; 347. 17 *in persecutione militia, in pace conscientia coronatur,* 734. 17, &c.; 256. 5 *inpunitum diu non fuit . . . dissimulatae conscientiae crimen,* 283 17 *admonemur quod peccatores sumus . . . ut conscientiae suae animus recordetur,* 474. 11, 739. 19, &c. *Bene sibi conscius* occurs 260. 5, 549. 4; *male sibi conscius* 678. 8, 683. 7.

[3] The verb in 308. 15, 730. 14 in addition to Hartel's instance from *Ep.* 22 (Lucianus).

Scriptural *dormire* is fairly common; *dormitio* is only used for peace after death, 466. 19, 467. 2. But usually words are chosen which simply convey the thought of departure; *abscedere* 636. 12, *decedere* 654. 3, *excedere* 304. 13, 466. 17, and often, and *recedere* 3c9. 20, &c., are all used absolutely[1]; *excedere a* or *de mundo, istinc*, &c. is also common; *de mundo recedentes* occurs 319. 9. *Exire* 730 14 *exire de saeculo*, &c., 300. 21, 26, 308. 18, &c.[2]; *perire*, of a Christian's death, perhaps only 307. 11; *transire ad immortalitatem* 503. 21. *Proficisci ad Dominum* 731. 21, cf. 339. 6, *transgredi ad immortalitatem* 310. 22, seem not to be repeated. The corresponding nouns are *excessus* and *exitus*, with and without *de saeculo*, &c. Of these the latter is the more common, though *excedere* is much more frequent than *exire*. *Transitus* and *transgressus* stand together, 310. 24, 25 (cf. 192. 21 *transgressus* of the entry upon a new life in Baptism); *profectio* 833. 6, *profectio et translatio* 311. 14, borrowed from the Biblical *transferri* used of Enoch, *ib.* 16, 20; *redditio* occurs 394. 26[3]. The curious *excidium*, which has almost a literature to itself, is used 312. 22; see p. 299. To die before another is *praecedere* 695. 6, 828. 7, *ante se mittere* 585. 16, *praemittere* 586. 6: cf. 282. 13. *Resurgere* is used of man in the Scriptural manner; *corpore redeunte* 16. 3. Concerning burial there is no noteworthy language; *cimiterium* is used of a Roman place of burial, 840. 9, cf. *Acta*, § 1 (cxi. 9); in 740. 20 *apud profana sepulcra depositos* is the language of a letter from Spain, not that of Cyprian.

The dead are commemorated at the altar; the *oblatio* is made for them, including the martyrs, and the Sacrifice

---

[1] So *cedere* in the Roman *Ep.* 8 (486. 18); *recedente spiritu* 559 6, also Roman; *recessit* absolute on a tomb, *C. I. L.* 8. 2010, for *obiit*. There is a valuable collection of terms for death, Christian and heathen, in A. Kubler's article on the Latinity of African Inscriptions in Wolfflin's *Archiv*, 8. 183, which shows that these forms of speech were by no means exclusively Christian. I have found this article a valuable supplement to my own reading of *C. I. L.* 8.

[2] *Exire* occurs in *Pass. Perp.* 11 (twice) and 13 in this sense; it seems to be absent in Tertullian.

[3] Cf. *redditio episcopi urbici* in the heading given by most MSS. to *Ep.* 9.

offered, 466. 19, 467. 2, 503. 14, 583. 10. At the altar the name of the deceased is pronounced 466. 20; the *anniuersaria commemoratio* of martyrs in 583. 12 no doubt took the same form. *Deprecatio* on behalf of the deceased is also mentioned 467. 3, but it is not clear whether this is distinct from the naming at the altar; the *aut* need not be disjunctive. But *frequentetur* would appear to indicate that there was, for a Christian who died a natural death, one funeral celebration of the Eucharist, and afterward for some time a mention of his name in the usual service. *Deprecatio* is not spoken of in the case of the martyrs.

The true life is *uita*; 370. 4 *hic uita aut amittitur aut tenetur*, 288. 1, 526. 5, and often. *Vitalis* in the sense of 'life-giving' is also frequent; *aqua uitalis* 188. 14, 219. 20, &c., *remedia* 254. 9, *praecepta* 189. 24, *fontes* 786. 12, &c.; so also *uiuere, Deo uiuere, in Deo uiuere* 187. 4, 283. 11, 370. 2, 753. 5, &c.; *uiuidus cultus = aeternus* 16. 1; *uiuentes episcopi* 726. 4. *Viuificare* in the senses both of 'giving life,' as 370. 17, and 'restoring to life,' as 275. 17, is common; *uiuificatio* 394. 9, &c. *Caelum* is varied once, at least, by the Biblical *caeli* 658. 27, and by *caelestia*, also Biblical, 204. 4. Neither of these is in a Scriptural context. *Regnum caelorum* is common, and *regnum* also without definition, e. g. 432. 15; see Hartel's *Index Verborum*: *regna caelorum* 394. 10; *superna*, at least four times, 362. 19, 392. 27, 428. 19, 579. 2[1]. *Paradisus* occurs 390. 10, 829. 19, and in a few other passages. *Refrigerium*, also Biblical, is used occasionally, e. g. 829. 26; but Cyprian never employs Tertullian's *refrigerare*. *Consummare, consummatio* are frequent, 379. 5, 489. 3, &c.; *Consummator* (sc. *Christus*) only 242. 6.

§ 28. It remains to speak of the enemies of the Church, *diabolus, saeculum, haeretici*, &c. *Diabolus*, of course, is common, but Cyprian, with his usual dislike of Greek words, more often paraphrases the name. *Aduersarius* is the most

---

[1] *Superna*, I think, occurs only once in Tert.; *Scorp.* 10 (167. 8 Reiff.). His words for heaven are the same as Cyprian's, but *paradisus* is much more common.

common substitute; 289. 18, 580. 7, &c., *Inimicus* somewhat less frequent, e. g. 211. 9; *Aduersarius et Inimicus*, together by pleonasm, 667. 20; *Aduersarius uetus et hostis antiquus* 317. 20. Both are used as actual substantives, and with attributes; *expugnator Inimicus* 201. 18; cf. 249. 10, &c. *Malus* = ὁ πονηρός is used 286. 6, 287. 13, &c., but less often than by Tertullian. *Malignus* is not used by Cyprian. It has been already mentioned that he never has *Satan* or *Satanas*. *Immundus spiritus* (cf. *Pass. Perp.* 21) is opposed to *Spiritus Sanctus* 645. 12, and is elsewhere used for *diabolus*, but more commonly is in the plural. *Serpens* occurs several times, 210. 1, 373. 15, &c., but *draco* is absent. Cyprian is apparently the inventor of the adjective *serpentinus* 431. 15, 806. 9. Evil spirits are *immundi spiritus* often, *immundi et erratici spiritus* 7. 16 (cf. *spiritu erroris abreptus* 211. 2), *spiritus nequam* 765. 1 and in *Ep.* 75 (817. 10), *peccatores et apostatae angeli* 197. 26. *Daemonia* seems to occur only 645. 11, *daemon* not at all[1]. For the ejection of these spirits Cyprian never uses *exorcizare*; he leaves it to the speakers in the *Sententiae*, though he is obliged to use the recognized *exorcista*. He gives instead rhetorical descriptions of the exorcist's work, *flagellare, urere, torquere*[2], &c., without any word for the actual command to depart. *Adiurare* occurs only once, 361. 18, and in *Quod Id.* 25. 3. Diabolical action is described with much variety, *conflictatio, infestatio, incursatio, laqueus, labes, uenenum, funus, adulator, ueterator, praeuaricator, feralis, funestus, letalis, circumuenire, grassari, deicere, auertere, euertere,* &c. *Inferi* is the normal name for hell, 362. 19, 636. 8, 647. 12, &c.; *gehenna* occurs several times, the only Hebrew word used by Cyprian which he could have avoided, e.g. 483. 8, 689. 9. But he prefers

[1] In *Quod Id.* both are found, 23. 15, 16 and 24. 4; *daemon* also in *Ep.* 75 (817. 8), and *daemoniacus* in *Sent.* 1 (436. 16). Tertullian uses *daemon* and *daemonium* indifferently, but avoids the forms *daemoniorum* and *daemonibus*. I have only noticed these four times and once respectively.

[2] Cf. *C. I. L.* 8. 2756 *carminibus defixa iacuit ... ut eius spiritus ui extorqueretur quam naturae redderetur.* Here *extorquere* must stand for *eicere*. It is a heathen monument to a wife. The conduct of the demon is described in language very like that in which Cyprian speaks of the exorcist, e.g. 361. 18, 764. 15.

The Language of St. Cyprian. 287

to paraphrase; *poenalis flamma* 665. 8, *ardens semper gehenna et uiuacibus flammis uorax poena* 368. 16 [1], &c. He does not use *tartarus*, though it is employed by Tertullian and by Novatian in *Ep.* 30 (555. 19).

§ 29. *Saeculum* is the usual word for the world, in the theological sense, as translating κόσμος, but there are a number of exceptions, where *mundus* appears; 363. 22, 365. 21, 397. 16, &c.; *saeculum et mundus* pleonastic 250. 1, 312. 4. If Haussleiter[2] is right in making *saeculum* in this sense distinctively African, Cyprian's use of *mundus* may be derived from the Baptismal formula, which no doubt was used exactly as it had been brought from Italy; 406. 3 *qui diabolo et mundo renuntiauimus* appears to be a clear allusion to it. *Terra* is used once only in this sense, 501. 5; cf. the argument of *Dom. Or.* § 17. The adjective *saecularis* constantly occurs, with *saeculariter* (103. 22, &c.); *terrenus* also often, *terrestris* at least twice, 7. 7, 244. 22, and cf. 411. 8; *mundanus* never.

The people of the world are, as already mentioned in § 8, *genus humanum* as contrasted with the *diuinum genus*. In the *Testimonia* they are called simply *gentes*, and also in *Ep.* 63 (704. 2, 711. 3, 6[3]). *Exterae gentes* occurs only 740. 20, and is not Cyprian's own, but the language of the Spanish letter whose contents he is reciting. Is it the case that the remoter churches used archaic language through their isolation, when terms had changed in the more central? We have seen that *hypodiaconus* only was used at Carthage, while *subdiaconus* has been introduced at Rome[4]. *Allophyli* occurs once in the *Testimonia* (83. 19); *alienigena* four times; once in the

---

[1] Cf. *uermium edax poena* 410. 9.

[2] In *Acta Sem. Erlang.* iii. p. 432, on the Palatine version of Hermas. *Mundus* is even rarer in Tertullian than in Cyprian.

[3] An additional evidence, if one were needed, for its being among the earliest of Cyprian's writings, composed before his style was formed.

[4] According to Haussleiter's article, cited above, in the older and, as he says, African version of Hermas, *gentes* or *exterae gentes* is almost constant. We see that Cyprian only uses *gentes* in his earliest writings, and *exterae gentes* never. *Nationes* also is avoided, though it stood in Cyprian's Bible; see Koffmane, p. 23.

Testimonia (83. 25), once in this reproduction of the Spanish letter, 740. 21, and twice in indirect citation of Scripture, 342. 2, 366. 22. It is thrice cited from Malachi 4. 1. It is to be noticed that, though *alienigena* occurs sparingly in the Vulgate as revised by Jerome, it is very common in the books where the old version has been left untouched. None of these words, then, are used by Cyprian after he had formed his style. He confined himself to *ethnicus* (775. 21, &c.) and *gentilis*. The change that was passing over the language of the Church may be seen in the rarity of *ethnicus*, though that seems the most common word in Tertullian for 'heathen[1].' Even in the titles to the *Testimonia*, where Cyprian has used so many archaic words, only *gentilis* is found. There seems to be no other synonym in Cyprian; *profanus* is only descriptive. Though the word is Biblical, yet it is not common either in Scripture or in Tertullian, and Cyprian in all probability borrowed it from his knowledge of classical literature. He usually reserves it for heretics, but *profanus arbiter, templa, dei* are found 3. 11, 399. 4, 411. 7, and the word 366. 4, 23 of heathens.

Idolum is constantly used, and also, though less commonly, *simulacrum*; *figmentum* occurs thrice (362. 15, 399. 5, 411. 8), as in Novatian, *Trin.* 3, and Tertullian, *Jud.* 1; it was perhaps frequent in the Old Latin; it still stands in Vulg. Sap. 14. 16. *Idolatra* occurs 645. 19, *idolatria* often[2]. *Ara* is used 242. 24, &c., *altare*, for the sake of variety, of a heathen altar, 243. 1, but never again. For these words see § 16. There is nothing remarkable about the words used for heathen worship; *sacrificia celebrare* 673. 15, *sacrificare idolis* 242. 13, *sacrificantes* 238. 5, &c. *Adscendere* stands alone 242. 11, *ad-*

---

[1] *Gentilis* is rare in Tertullian except in *Ad Ux.* and *Cult. Fem.*, where he uses it freely. He constantly uses *nationes*, very rarely *gentes*. *Allophylus* and *extraneus* are occasional variants for his normal *ethnicus*.

[2] So these forms are certainly to be spelt; see especially 325. 22, and 740. 12, 22; in these two last instances Hartel's MSS. have no variant. Cf. Wölfflin in his *Archiv*, 5. 496 and 8. 6, Miodoński on *De Aleatt.* 5. 3, and Koffmane, p. 37. Tertullian uses the full form (yet cf. 368. 4 Reiff.), and in Lucifer also (see Hartel's Article in Wölfflin's *Archiv*, 3. 23), the MS. has *idololatria*, &c. more often than the syncopated form.

The Language of St. Cyprian. 289

scendere Capitolium 254. 16 ; cf. 242. 19, 531. 19. This would seem to have become a synonym for the offering of sacrifice. A worshipper of idols is often called *sacrilegus*[1], usually in rhetorical contrast to *sacerdos, sacrificium*, &c. 253. 22, 399. 5, &c.

§ 30. The trouble caused by the heathen to the Church is *persecutio, tribulatio* or *pressura*. The two last are renderings of θλίψις from Scripture. *Pressura*[2], though its use is not always precise, is more definitely connected with persecution than *tribulatio*. The descriptions of confessorship and martyrdom as *aliud baptisma* (i. e. *alterum*) or *sanguinis baptisma* (319. 4, 796. 1, cf. *Pass. Perp.* 18. 21, &c.), *purificatio confessionis* 578. 26 (cf. 786. 24 of Baptism), *tormenta quae martyras Dei consecrant et ipsa passionis probatione sanctificant* 481. 12, and the like, belong rather to Theology than to the study of language. That which is confessed is *nomen* or *nomen Christi*; usually the former, e. g. 103. 23. 278. 3, 795. 18, &c. The language used concerning modes of torture, &c. does not belong to this subject ; it is naturally often rhetorical. Prison, for instance, is rarely *carcer* ; *hospitium carceris* 494. 2, 577. 22, *poenalis locus* 577. 12, *poenale receptaculum* 578. 15, and other paraphrases take its place. There is a great variety of language for the martyrs' reward, in such *Epp.* as 28, 37, 38, 39, 76, which need not be given here. The characteristic word is *palma* 402. 15, 493. 20, 831. 24, &c., which takes the place of the *brauium* of Tertullian. Cyprian read it, and not *brauium*, in 1 Cor. 9. 24 (141. 5, according to the true text, 330. 1, 493. 7).

All who stand firm under persecution are *stantes* ; those

---

[1] Cf. *De Aleatt.* 7, with Harnack's note, p. 23, who says that *sacrilegium = idololatria* is common in Sulpicius Severus.

[2] This word, which Jerome has almost banished from the Vulgate, where it now stands in only seven passages—six in the N. T., which Jerome probably overlooked, one in the Apocrypha, and none in the O. T.—must have been as common in the Old Latin as *tribulatio*. In Cyprian its common use is of persecution, e. g. 241. 23, 833 14, of want, less often, as 291. 26, 479. 4, and also of trouble generally. It is used literally of overcrowding, 534. 13, by Lucianus. The Roman Christians still used *thlibomeni*, 487. 21, as in Cornelius' letter in Eus. *H. E.* 6. 43. 11, and *Canon. Apost.* 22.

290 The Style and Language of St. Cyprian.

who suffer, whether fatally or not, are *confessores* (*confitentes* once, 615. 5) or *martyres*. *Testis* (cf. *Vita, init. Cyprianus . . . testis Dei gloriosus*) does not seem to be used. *Confessor* and *martyr* are used equally often, and quite indifferently [1]; the pleonastic *martyres et confessores* 513. 5, 520. 17, &c. *Confiteri, confessio* stand both alone and with *Christum, Christi* dependent. *Confessio nominis* 653. 22, &c. *Martyrium* or *martyria facere* occurs several times, perhaps on the analogy of *stipendia facere*; *martyria edere* once, 742. 3; *martyrium tollere* 653. 12. In 698. 3 is the otiose *confessionis martyria*, and 260. 7 *uirtutum martyria* [2]. *Passio* and *passiones* are frequent.

The *uirtutes, laudes, gloriae,* all meaning meritorious actions, of the confessors are often mentioned, e. g. 547. 3, 577. 1, 578. 12 [3]. But the characteristic virtue of the confessor is *tolerantia* 204. 20, 415. 14, &c. The wealth of epithets for the confessors is great; *gloriosus, inlibatus, inmaculatus, inconcussus, inmotus,* &c. *Beatus*, used in addressing them, has already been mentioned; cf. 576. 22 *beatum facit prima et una confessio*. Was it a recognized title?

Exile, either voluntarily endured to escape death, or inflicted as a punishment, is often mentioned. The sufferer is always *extorris* [4], *profugus*, &c. being only used for variety, and *exul*, I think, never. Bishops are sentenced to *relegatio*; Lucius of Rome, for instance, 695. 19. If this instance stood alone it would be a strong confirmation of the statement of

---

[1] Cf. Lightfoot's *Apostolic Fathers*, ii. p. 26 f. 'The Decian persecution would seem to have been instrumental in fixing this distinction between martyrs and confessors.' The traces of it in Cyprian are very slight; 627. 8 *Moyse tunc adhuc confessore nunc iam martyre*, and Nemesianus' description in *Ep.* 77 (834. 15) of martyrdom as *magna confessio*. *Confessor* and *confessio* are very rare in Tertullian; they were perhaps only just coming into use when he wrote, through a popular dislike of the Greek equivalents.

[2] While *confessio* has almost lost the sense of 'confession of sin,' *exhomologesis* has lost that of 'confessing,' in the sense of recognizing, God's glory. Yet it must have had it in Cyprian's Bible (260. 10, cf. *Test.* 3. 114), though he preferred to take it in the meaning which he always gives to the word.

[3] *Laus* in this sense also occurs in the singular, e.g 621. 8. Cyprian may have remembered Virgil, *Aen*. 5. 355 *primam merui qui laude coronam*.

[4] There is some evidence, e.g. 507. 2, 616. 16, 633. 11, for Cyprian's having used the vulgar form *extorrens*.

the Felician catalogue that Lucius was born *patre purpureo*, since *relegatio* affected only the higher classes. Yet both in the *Vita* and in the *Acta* Cyprian is sentenced not to *relegatio* but to *exilium*, while we read in 731. 21 of a large number of bishops *in exilium relegati*. If the episcopate could be desired for worldly reasons, as Cyprian says in *Laps.* 6 and *Ep.* 65. 3, they could hardly be among the *tenuiores* of Roman law, and subject to the heavier punishments of such[1]. Voluntary exile is *cedere*, 244. 13, *secedere*, 244. 10, 14, and often, *recedere* still more commonly, 570. 15, 659. 20, &c.

In connexion with confessorship Cyprian uses many metaphors, especially those of sacrifice, of warfare, of the arena and the race. Martyrs are *uictimae* 698. 4, *hostiae* 830. 23, *hostiae et uictimae* 652. 24; cf. 561. 18 in the Roman *Ep.* 31. The Church is *castra Christi, caelestia*, &c., often certainly, perhaps always, in the sense of army, not of camp; e. g. 363. 12, 693. 11, 806. 5; yet cf. 490. 16. Confession is constantly *proelium* (492. 8 *proeliatores et adsertores sui nominis*), *certamen*, e. g. 545. 7 ff., &c. Christians are *commilitones* 686. 15; *militare Deo* occurs 297. 15, *militia* for the Christian warfare, campaign, conduct in battle, is frequent, 649. 13, 658. 28, &c.[2] *Commeatus* of respite from martyrdom occurs thrice, 494. 22, 581. 20, 632. 24[3].

The Christian conflict is also compared to that of the gladiator. In 498. 12 the devil is seen in vision as a *retiarius*.

---

[1] Probably, therefore, the possibilities of suffering for Cornelius mentioned in *Ep.* 55. 6 (630. 21 ff.) are only rhetoric. In the hostile *Ep.* 8 (486. 1) the Roman clergy call Cyprian a *persona insignis*. They seem to be magnifying his fault in retiring by alluding to his position in society, which would have saved him, at the worst, from such punishment as humble Christians endured. Yet in *Ep.* 76 (829. 13, 17) we find bishops suffering from *infamia uincula, infamia*. This is the only use of the legal term *infamia* in connexion with this persecution. Some of the bishops may have been of humble position, but legality was not considered in Valerian's persecution. Clergy of all orders were being treated as convicts in the mines.

[2] *Militia* is equivalent to *exercitus* in 545. 8 *caelestis militiae signa mouistis*, and 657. 24. *Miles* is collective 491. 21.

[3] It is used in the meaning of recovery from sickness, 309. 1, 14; so also in Sen. *Ep.* 54. 1.

In 664. 23 the *galea* is described, covering the whole head, and seems to be that of a gladiator. The very term *stantes* is identical with, if not borrowed from, the gladiatorial name for the victor [1]. The gladiator's food is used as an illustration in the Roman *Ep.* 31 (557. 18) *ita illas (literas) uoto esuriente suscepimus ut ad certamen inimici ex illis nos satis pastos et saginatos gaudeamus*; literally, of a gladiator in *Ad Don.* 9. 1. Further passages, such as 15. 20 *cum semel pectus caelestis sagina saturauerit*, 401. 17 *diebus quadraginta ieiunat per quem ceteri saginantur*, Tert. *Res. Carn.* 8 *caro corpore et sanguine Christi uescitur, ut et anima de Deo saginetur*, suggest that there may have been in the Old Latin Bible a use of *saginare* as meaning to strengthen or satisfy, in such passages, for instance, as Matt. 5. 6. But there seems to be no evidence of any such use; there is certainly none in Tertullian or Cyprian. It seems therefore more probable that the word, even in these cases, comes from the same metaphor [2]. Apart from this use the word is employed by Cyprian in its usual classical sense of gluttony, 259. 6, 468. 20. The *agon* [3] or *certamen* which was the object of the *spectaculum* (all these words are equally common) was often athletic, but sometimes clearly gladiatorial; e. g. 526. 15 *acies adhuc geritur et agon cottidie celebratur*, 578. 13 *agon unus sed multiplici proeliorum numerositate congestus*. In the latter the confessor has to meet a succession of fresh opponents, like the *ter fortis* of Quint. *Decl.* 271. Indeed Cyprian's use of *fortis* seems generally to be the technical one of Quintilian's *Declamations*, in which it is common, as also in Quint. *Inst.* 7. 7, not merely meaning brave, but implying that the courage has been shown in action, and the reward earned [4]. The

[1] See the examples from inscriptions collected by Friedlander, *Darstellungen*, ii. 363, 518.

[2] For the gladiatorial use cf. Apul. *Met.* 4. 14, where the robbers are described as *pulpis saginantes* (intransitive) in preparation for their *instans militia*; Quint. *Decl.* 9. 5 (cited by Mayor on Juv. 11. 20) *alebat deuotum corpus grauior omni fame sagina*. For the word cf. Koffmane, p. 99.

[3] Cf. Is 7. 13 in 74. 4, 492. 21, and for the subject Origen, *Protrept.* 18.

[4] The use of so unchristian an illustration as that of the gladiator, if it did

general language of training, running, receiving a crown, &c. in such passages as 317. 19, 493. 3, 663. 18, &c. is, of course, in the main Pauline, but has been much developed. In 580. 4 there is an allusion to some arrangement of the games. The confessor passes through a *geminus agon*; first *cursus* and then a *certamen fortius*. Is this wrestling?

There are several notices of the reverence paid to Martyrs. The date of their death is recorded, 503. 14, though Cyprian never calls it their *natalis*, and *commemorationes* or *memoriae* (the words are probably synonymous, *memoria* not having the later sense of 'tomb') held for them, 503. 15, 583. 12. Sacrifice is offered for them as for others who are deceased; cf. pp. 267, 284, and not simply in memory of their victory.

For martyrdom as a *baptisma sanguinis* see especially *Ep.* 73. 21, 22, and p. 319. 5 ff. The thought is common both in Cyprian and Tertullian, e. g. *Scorp.* 12, *Bapt.* 16 (174. 6, 214. 14 Reiff.).

The opposite to *confessio, confiteri* is *professio* 256. 25 (cf. Novatian, 550. 24), *profiteri* 238. 25, and perhaps 842. 5. Though *lapsus* is constant for a fallen Christian, *labi* does not occur except in compound tenses, as 541. 7, 650. 18, &c. *Apostatare* is used only 652. 10; it is, no doubt, simply an accident that *apostata* refers only to heretics, 632. 10, 647. 16; cf. 197. 26, 825. 18. The downfall itself is *lapsus* 648. 15, &c., but more often *ruina* 239. 18, 501. 16, 721. 17, &c. Metaphors from death, disease, shipwreck, &c. are common. Many have been given already in § 25; much of this language is also used in reference to schism: see the next section. The kinds of *lapsi* mentioned are *libellatici*[1], of whose crime

not arise from the circumstances of common life, must have come from the Stoics. Friedlander. *Darstellungen*, ii. 400 n., cites from De Rossi a Christian vessel found at Tunis with the figure of a victorious *thrax* or *retiarius* upon it. De Rossi says that it is a symbol of the triumphant soul; Friedlander would have it to be a charioteer. Whatever archaeological reasons he may have, no weight can be attached to his further argument that Christians would never have used such a symbol. Cyprian, we have seen, had no such scruple. For his relation to Seneca see p. 202, and cf. Tert. *Mart.* 1.

[1] *Libellus* is used by Cyprian for his own treatises, 36. 7, 623. 16, 798. 19,

a variety is that of those *qui accepta fecissent* 551. 3 (Novatian), whatever the exact meaning of that may be; *turificati* and *sacrificati*. These names are perfectly definite in their employment and belong to history rather than to a study of language.

§ 31. *Haeresis* and *schisma* are identical terms in Cyprian, though constantly used, after his pleonastic fashion, together[1]. *Haereticus*[2] and *schismaticus* are equally constant and identical in meaning. *Haeresin, schisma facere* are also normal, 746. 6, 754. 17, &c. Cyprian tried several Latin substitutes, but apparently was not satisfied with any; *discretio et separatio* 603. 2, *discessio* 619. 15, *schisma et discidium* 666. 20, *discidium compaginis, fraternitatis, unitatis* 231. 10, 604. 16, 672. 8, *discordia* (not moral, but actual schism) 222. 7, 642. 24[3]; cf. *diuortium* 215. 8. The authors of such division are *diuersa pars* 600. 1, i.e. hostile, cf. *conuenticula diuersa* 220. 24; *discrepans*[4] *factio* 602. 7; *discordes* often, though *dis-*

&c; of a letter from the lapsed, claiming communion, in *Ep* 33 (568. 3), but there is some doubt of the genuineness of this *Ep.*; of the letters of the confessors readmitting the *lapsi* to communion, 523. 19, &c., which are also called *litterae*, 541. 6, 9; finally, of these certificates given by the magistrate that a Christian had sacrificed, 341. 19, &c. The use in *Ep.* 33 resembles the Egyptian *libellus* lately discovered; see Harnack in *Theol. Litztg.* 1894, p. 38. The thing existed in Tertullian's time, though he does not name it; cf. Kolberg p. 146.

[1] Cf. 598 16, 746. 6, where *haeresis* clearly means schism. The very fact that they are used together is in Cyprian's style an evidence that they are identical; cf. *sauciati et uulnerati, preces et orationes*, and so many more. The only passages where there seems to be a distinction of meaning are a few in which they are joined by *uel—uel*, instead of *et—et*, but there are so many instances in Cyprian in which *uel* is not disjunctive that no argument can be drawn from these; besides them there are only 614. 14 *schismaticus immo haereticus furor*, and 805. 1 *cum uero nulla omnino haeresis sed neque aliquod schisma habere salutaris baptismi sanctificationem foris possit*, neither of which is more than rhetoric.

[2] Cornelius seems to use *haeresiacus* 611. 13, 612. 14, which Cyprian rejects.

[3] Jerome, *Ep.* 94. 2, ventures on *scissura*; cf. Vulgate, 1 Cor. 11. 18; Cyprian and Tertullian do not cite this text. Cyprian only has the word from 3 Reg. 11. 31, in 216. 2. In *Sent.* 5 (440. 1) occurs *qui diuisionem faciunt, hoc est schismaticos et haereticos*. The Echternach Gospels stand alone in reading *discisio* for σχίσμα in Joh. 7. 43; Vulgate *dissensio*. There was clearly a strong desire for a Latin word.

[4] The verb is used absolutely 497. 14, 529. 2.

The Language of St. Cyprian. 295

cordans and *discordiosus* are not found in the special sense. Their work is constantly *scindere ecclesiam, unitatem,* &c. 224. 11, 605. 6, &c., *rescindere* 642. 24, *discerpere* 231. 11, 604. 14, *distrahere scindere laniare* 598. 20. *Abscedere* 631. 21, *discedere* 733. 2, &c., and especially *recedere* 777. 21, &c., are common, as are *segregare se* 214. 20, 745. 5, &c., *foras egredi* 757. 16, *exire, derelinquere ecclesiam* and similar phrases. *Rebellio* is frequent; *rebellare contra pacem*, &c., 472. 4, 592. 25, and often. *Conspiratio, seditio, factio, seductio* (725. 16), are also common. Beside these Cyprian uses *aemuli, aemulantes, aemulatio discissa*[1] 222. 3, 598. 14, 604. 14, &c.; *praeuaricatio* 213. 17, *praeuaricator*[2] 742. 6, 759. 3, 786. 13, in all cases combined with *proditor*. Generally speaking all the language used or suitable for evil spirits or heathens, traitors or madmen, is bestowed upon heretics; perhaps the most common terms are *profanus, adulter*[3] and *sacrilegus*; the three are combined, 745. 12. *Praesumptio* (add to Hartel's list 747. 24, 801. 16, 807. 12, and in another sense 459. 14), *pertinacia*[4] 600. 2, *tumor, stupor, furor, uenenum* are characteristic terms. *Maligni*[5] *et detrahentes* 629. 3, *perditi, perditio, perdere et perire* are very common, as are the metaphors of *parricidium* and *naufragium*.

For the meeting of heretics Cyprian avoids *synagoga* (twice in *Ep.* 75, 819. 24, 820. 25). He twice uses *conuenticulum* instead; *conuenticula diuersa* 220. 23, *conuenticulum perditae factionis* 683. 6.

§ 32. That Cyprian's list of Greek words is short, and that

---

[1] For *aemulus = hostis* see Rönsch, *It V.* p. 338. *Discissa aemulatio* must be for *aemulatio schismatica*; so *error scissus* 599. 1 = *schismatis*.

[2] These words, with *praeuaricari*, are used several times, generally of the effect of a bad life, 198. 23, 309. 27, 388. 17, 423. 7, 427. 7; *praeuaricatio ueritatis = lapsus* 592. 13; *praeuaricatio = haeresis* is used by Cornelius also, 612. 15.

[3] See § 9, and cf. *uitiare* 614. 10.

[4] Does this mean cruelty, in deserting their mother? For *pertinax* in this sense see p. 305.

[5] This is an indirect evidence that in Cyprian's time *malignus = diabolus* was in use; cf. 425. 2.

296 The Style and Language of St. Cyprian.

there are few for which he has not attempted to provide a substitute, has already been said on p. 195. There is only one Greek ecclesiastical term, *symbolum*, which appears to occur for the first time in him (756. 7, cf. 818. 10), and he only uses it once. It is no doubt a mere accident that no earlier instance has survived. Cyprian's object was not to introduce, but to banish, Greek words. In the preceding pages the ecclesiastical words have been set out in detail. It may suffice here to set them together without further comment.

Those for which Cyprian provides no substitute are *acoluthus, angelus, angelicus, apostolus* (also of messengers of evil 642. 17), *blasphemus, blasphemia, blasphemare, cathedra, catholicus, clerus, clericus, ecclesia, ecclesiasticus, ecstasis, euangelium, euangelicus, exorcismus, exorcista* (never *exorcizare*), *hypodiaconus* (leaving *subdiaconus* to Rome), *idolatra, idolatria, laicus, presbyter, presbyterium, conpresbyter, propheta, propheticus, pseudochristus, pseudoepiscopus* (*pseudoapostolus* and *pseudopropheta* are words of Stephanus, not of Cyprian), *zelus* and *zelare* (never the deponent). There are only two other Greek words of Christian sense which he freely uses, *agon* (with *agonisticus*), and *petra* (see pp. 292, 280). A few Biblical words, as *botruus* 578. 1, 705. 20, 754. 9, *grabatus* 762. 16, *lepra* 226. 25, *leprosus* 671. 3, &c., *moechus* 638. 11, *patriarcha* 308. 9, &c., *zizania* 622. 15, 16, a few more which had been thoroughly adopted in Latin, classical or post-classical, as *aphronitra* pl. = 'cakes of soap' 761. 4 (cf. Treb. Poll *Gall.* 6. 5), *authenticus* 489. 16 (Tert., Jct.), *catasta* 581. 1 (see p. 270), *chorus* 313. 27, *collyrium* 384. 15, *conchylium* (= *murex*) 197. 18, *cynocephalus* 360. 6, *stibium* 384. 15; *tropaeum, tyrannicus,* &c., need not be noticed. *Plasmare* 805. 15, *plastica* 198. 7, *protoplastus* 190. 15 (also in Novatian, *Trin.* 8) are reminiscences of Tertullian; *plasma* 468. 12, not used by Tertullian, probably comes direct from Irenaeus.

Cyprian twice shows that he had some knowledge of Greek. In 762. 9 he ridicules his opponents who used the word

The Language of St. Cyprian. 297

clinici, and in 765. 18 adopts the humorous *peripatetici* in contrast; similarly in 694. 3 he contrasts *sophia dominica* with *saecularis philosophia*.

But the most important group of Greek words are those of Church use for which Cyprian employs, more or less frequently, a Latin substitute. These are:—

agape only *Test.* 3. 3 *tit.*, coupled with the synonymous *dilectio* [1].
allophyli only 83. 19 (*Test.* 3. 16). See p. 287.
apostata, apostatare, see p. 293. Much less common than *desertor* and other Latin terms.
baptismus, baptisma, baptismum; see § 15. Cyprian's normal use is *baptisma* nom. acc., with oblique cases from *baptismus*, and plural *baptismata*. No other plural forms are found. But 781. 20 *baptismatis* without variant, and 787. 22 *baptismate*, though there is much evidence for *baptismo*. There is no instance of nom. *baptismus*, and only, I think, 775. 15, 776. 7 for *baptismum* acc.; in the latter it is neuter, if the text may be trusted. In the *Sentt* there is one clear instance of the masc., two clearly neuter, twenty-six doubtful, twenty of *baptisma*. Tertullian wavers between these forms as much as Cyprian. *Baptisma*, abl., ought to be read 788. 8 and 796. 13, as in *Ep.* 75 (815. 11); cf. Koffmane, p. 36. *Baptizare* and *rebaptizare* are used without variant except in paraphrase. It has been already suggested that *tinctio, tinguere* are avoided, as Montanist words, and only used as descriptions of the heretical rite.
catecumenus 106. 18, 488. 2, 795. 16 (*catechizare* in *Ep.* 75 (823. 17)); *audiens* twice.
chrisma once only 768. 14, and there explained by *unctio*.
christianus, see p. 254; emphatic and comparatively rare.
daemon, daemonium; see p. 286. Almost always *immundi spiritus*, &c.
diabolus often, yet more frequently *inimicus*, &c.; see p. 285.
diaconus [2], *diaconium*; for these and for *minister, administratio* as probably equivalent, see p. 260.

---

[1] But there is strong evidence for *agape* having stood in Cyprian's Bible. It is used 114. 1, 115. 13, 116, 17, 133. 8 in Lord Crawford's MS. (8th cent.), as well as in the best of those cited by Hartel.

[2] With the exception of abl. *baptisma, diaconus* is the only Greek word with the form of which Cyprian took liberties; *diaconem* should perhaps be read in 618. 12; *diacones* 565. 11 (doubtful *ib.* 5), 839. 16, 840. 10; *diaconi-*

episcopus, episcopatus, coepiscopus; see p. 258. *Antistes* and *sacerdos* constantly. *Coepiscopus* seems to be a coinage of Cyprian's.

ethnicus rarely for *gentilis*; see p. 288.

eucharistia comparatively rare; see p. 266.

exhomologesis always except 258. 18, where *confessio* is used; see p. 282.

haeresis, haereticus constantly; for Latin synonyms see p. 294.

idolum is varied by *figmentum* and *simulacrum*; see p. 288.

martyr, martyrium indiscriminately with *confessor*, &c.; see p. 290.

prophetare 223. 17, 339. 26, elsewhere *praedicere*, &c.

scandalum (add to Hartel's list 474. 19, 508. 3) five times, *scandalizare* thrice; *offendiculum* perhaps only 304. 14.

schisma, schismaticus constantly; for variants see p. 294.

synagoga only *Test.* 1. 20 *tit.* In the sense of 'heretical assembly' *conuenticulum* takes its place 220. 23, 683. 6.

typus often, yet more often *imago*, &c.; see § 7.

Noteworthy Greek words used by other writers in the *Epp.* and *Sententiae* are—*catechizare* 823. 17, *cimiterium* (of a Roman burial-place) 840. 9[1], *daemoniacus* 436. 16, *exorcizare* 436. 16, &c. (confined to *Sentt.*), *petrarium* (a conjecture) 534. 18, *pseudobaptizatus* 438. 4, *tartarus* 555. 19, *thlibomeni* 487. 21, *zelotypus* 533. 13.

§ 33. The length of this paper makes it impossible to do more than select out of Cyprian's general vocabulary a few of the most remarkable words; and especially those which appear for the first time in his writings. Beside the ordinary stock of words of a writer of the third century, common to Apuleius, Tertullian[2], Justin, the Old Latin Bible, &c., there

bus usually in the addresses (*diaconis, Epp.* 14, 39). See Ronsch, *It. V.* p. 262. Διάκων is found in third-century Greek Inscriptions, Pagan and Christian (Ramsay, *Church in the Roman Empire*, p. 442; Lightfoot, *Ignatius*, 1. 501). Conversely πάτρων in Theoph. *Ad Autol.* 3. 27 and often in inscriptions.

[1] Cited from a despatch from Rome; in the *Acta* of Cyprian § 1 it is used by the proconsul Paternus. Koffmane p. 31 has overlooked it in Tert. *de An.* 51 (383. 16 Reiff.), perhaps the earliest instance.

[2] Oehler's Index to Tertullian is very imperfect. He omits, among others, these words for which Cyprian has been in several cases cited as the earliest authority;—*adhucusque, Jud.* 7 (Cyprian 495. 18, 679. 13, the first instances according to Thielmann in Wolfflin's *Archiv*, 6, p. 69); *deponere* = 'depose,'

The Language of St. Cyprian.

are many borrowed from classical poetry, of which some examples have already been given, and many found in Plautus and other early writers, which do not recur till the third century. All these classes of words are, with few exceptions, omitted here, as are those which have been previously discussed. Words which seem to be new in form are marked with an asterisk, those which are new in meaning with an obelus.

The most noteworthy substantives, arranged alphabetically according to declension, are:—

†*culturae* 646. 19. This may mean works of agriculture, though for the pl. in this sense Georges only cites Lucr. 5. 1448, whom Cyprian does not seem to have read. But his love for parallelism makes it more likely that it corresponds with the preceding clause, and means fields. In this sense Georges only cites Salvian, *Gub. Dei*, 7. 2 (157. 20 Pauly).

†*exultantia=gaudium* 832. 25. In Georges only in the sense of attack, and first in Gellius.

fauentia 576. 17=*fauor*. Only cited from Accius, tr. 510.

*inaudientia 569. 22, invented by Cyprian for alliteration.

**lupana = meretrix* 196. 14, 699. 25; also in *De Spect.* 5 (A. 8. 5). Cf. Wölfflin, in his *Archiv*, 1892, p. 8, and Haussleiter, *ib.* p. 145.

**commentarii=commentarienses* 841. 3. The latter is common enough, but Cyprian's form does not seem to occur again. But there is some manuscript evidence for *frumentarii*, which is read by Rigault and Fell.

*diaconium 617. 1; cf. p. 260, and Koffmane, p. 25 [1].

**excidium=mors* 312. 22, apparently an ἅπαξ λεγόμενον, derived from *excidere*; cf. *C.I.L.* 8. 9513 (from Caesarea Mauret.) *xlv annis uobis uixi, in xlvi excidi quando datum est.*

Fug. 1 (Cypr. 472. 6, 739. 23); *deuotio*='loyalty,' *Scorp.* 5 (Cypr. 631. 5, 660. 9); *mortalis* = 'deadly,' *Pud.* 19 *fin.* twice (Cypr. 407 21, 469. 3, 725. 16 and *de Aleatt.* 6. 11; cf. Hilgenfeld's edition, p. 73, and Ronsch *Beitr.* 2. 32); *numerositas Monog.* 4 (Cypr. 214, 5, &c); *quamdiu=donec, Idol.* 15, *Natl.* 1. 7, &c. (Cypr. 496. 15, 649. 21, 679. 3).

[1] If Hartel's almost certain conjecture in *De Aleatt* 3. 2 (improved by Miodoński in *Comment. Woelfflin*, p. 373 ff. to *in episcopium idem*) for *episcopi idem* be accepted, the parallel form is brought back from the age of Hilary, Aug. and *xii Abus.* almost to that of Cyprian.

Georges in the *Jahresbericht*, vol. 40, p. 126 gives the word this derivation, citing Prud. *Apoth* 607 for the sense of 'sunset.' But Thielmann (Wölfflin's *Archiv*, 1. p. 76) makes it a vulgar derivative from *excĭdere* for *excedere*, in the sense of *excessus*. He gives some of Rönsch's (*It. V.* p. 356) examples of *decidere*=*decedere* (i. e. *mori*), and adds others of his own; but this seems a less probable account. It would be more likely that the word is formed on the analogy of *discidium*, which often enough means no more than 'departure[1].'

†*fomentum*=*fomes* 10. 7, 194. 12, 591. 18, all pl. Arnob. 2. 62 (98. 3 Reiff.).

*inpiamentum 724. 13. Cf. Min. Fel. 28. 5 *inpiatis sacris*.

†*oblectamenta et inlecebrae*, certainly synonyms, 501. 4. For *oblectare* in this sense see Koffmane, p. 95.

††*trauersaria* 829. 21; omitted by Georges in the sense of 'fetters' or rather, perhaps, 'stocks.' Ducange cites Greg. Tur. *De Vita Patrum*, 7, Forcellini-De Vit only this passage.

uultum 259. 22 *neclecto capillo, uulto nubilo*. Hartel cites no variant, and this may therefore be a mere misprint. But in Apul. *Met.* 4. 25 (71. 30 Eyss.) *saeuiore uulto* is read without variant in Eyssenhardt's MSS.; and it is quite possible that Cyprian has chosen the rare form for uniformity of termination. Cf. Georges, *Lex. d. lat. Wortformen*[2].

Of the third declension the only class in which Cyprian displays much invention is that of verbal nouns in -*tio*.

*acerbatio (pl.) 600. 21; the only example in Georges. Rönsch, *It. V.* p. 79 cites Gloss. Cyrill.

†*adflictatio mali*='infliction' 685. 1. Georges only cites *Cod. Theod.* for this use.

*adunatio; add 712. 1 to Hartel's instances. Paucker, *Suppl.* cites Cassiod. and Boethius. Cyprian is the first Christian

---

[1] Cf. *exitium*, which in the third and fourth centuries had been weakened to a synonym of *exitus*=*mors*. Apul. *Met.* 5. 27 (95. 4 Eyss.) *mortis exitium* means no more than Cyprian's *mortis exitus* (502. 17, 632. 19). So also in Firm. Mat. *Err.* 2. 7 and 28. 13 *animaduersionis exitium* is exactly equivalent to *diuinae animaduersionis exitus* in 18 4. Cf. Oehler's note to Tert. i. 518.

[2] Cf. *amictum*, Novatian, *Trin.* 21 (16), which Georges, *Lex. d. lat. Wortformen* only cites from Isidore; and *sepultum fecit*=*sepulcrum*, C. I. L. 8. 9798 (Safar, Numidia), though this might be from *sepultus*. Georges has not the word.

writer to use the verb freely, though it occurs in Tert. *Pud.* 5 and is Biblical.

arcessitio = mors, see p. 283; *arcessitio dominica* 309. 19. It is curious that this word, which Cyprian uses five times, and Lucianus (534. 5) once, should not have been adopted by later writers.

†*auulsio* 304. 13 *de excedentibus caris funebris et tristis auulsio.* Paucker, *Subindenda*, cites from Paulin. Nol. *Ep.* 13. 8, and it is used by Tert. *Carn. Xti* 20 of physical separation.

calcatio 705. 19 *torcularis calcatio et pressura* from Old Latin, Es. 63. 2 (*ib.* l. 13). This word is omitted by Georges, and by Rönsch in *It. V., Beitr.*, and *Collect.*, but noticed by Paucker in his *Suppl.*

†*concarnatio*, *Test.* 2. 2 *tit.*; see p. 248. Though *incarnatus* is used by Novatian, *Trin.* 19, Cyprian has no such form. *Concarnatio* is used in another sense (from Mt. 19. 5) by Tert. *Monog.* 9.

†*conceptio perniciosa* 307. 29; sense invented to carry on the preceding *conceptum*.

corroboratio 386. 1. Not in Vulg. or Tert. Paucker, *Suppl.* gives 2 Pet. 3. 17 from Aug. (without reference) *ne decidatis . . . a corroboratione uestra* (Vulg. *firmitate*)[1].

†*detractatio*=calumny 689. 19. Paucker, *Suppl.* only cites Cassian, *Coll.* 9. 3.

†*dissimulatio*=delay 358. 23 *praedandi dissimulatio nulla, nulla cunctatio.* Since it is Cyprian's constant habit to say the same thing twice, there can be no reasonable doubt of the meaning. Cf. *dissimulare* in Virg. *Aen.* 4. 368, and Rönsch, *It. V.* p. 523.

†*examinatio* (metaphorical) 500. 4. Arnob., Ulpian, &c.; cf. Paucker, *Suppl.* The verb is so used 218. 18, 409. 22, 686. 18.

†*factio*='factiousness' 602. 21, 618. 12. Georges only cites Cassian, *Coll.* 22. 6.

---

[1] Other resemblances of Cyprian to 2 Pet. (i. e. words first found in both, and not again till much later), which suggest the thought that the Vulgate of this Epistle is the Old Latin, as in some other of the Catholic Epp., are *cognitio* (*Patris et Filii*) 790. 20, which in this connexion is found in the Vulgate only in 2 Pet., *incessabilis* 793. 10 and 2 Pet 2. 14 (it recurs in Hieron. *Ep.* 16. 2); but *indesinens* 394. 13 is the alternative reading in 2 Pet. 2. 14 of *Cod. Tolet.* (Rönsch, *It. V.* p. 226), and also first recurs in Cyprian.

incursatio 364. 2. Nonius, Heges.
interminatio 476. 2. See Rönsch, *Collect.* p. 37, and Paucker, *Suppl.*
†*ostensio=uisio* 651. 7, 17, 734. 2, all pl.; see p. 250.
palpatio = 'flattery' 569. 17. Plautus, Cassian, *Inst.* 10. 17, Interp. Orig. in Mt. 6. 4 (Paucker, *Kl. Beitr.*).
ploratio 369. 17; only cited from Aug. *Serm.*, but omitted by Regnier.
†*pullulatio* (metaphorical) 352. 16; cf. *pullulare* 224. 14, 806. 10. Paucker, *Subrelicta*, only cites this and Praedestinatus in this sense.
†*seminatio* (metaphorical) 642. 24, 689. 17, 788. 19; cf. *seminare* 352. 15, 577. 19, 618. 8.
†*tinctio*='heretical Baptism,' 772. 8, 800. 7, and in *Ep.* 75 (815. 20); see p. 264.

---

celsitas 583. 25; omitted by Georges, and even by Paucker.
†*mortalitas* = *pestis* 301. 12, &c., in *De Mort.* Cited by Georges only from the Chronologer of 354.
†*rusticitas*='agriculture' 646. 18. Cited in this sense only from Palladius, and in Cyprian no doubt used for epiploce with *rusticum* preceding. The word occurs in *Quod Id.* 2 (20. 7).

Beside these the following deserve mention :—

acceptor 692. 23; Wölfflin, in *Archiv*, 8. 123, cited only from Lucilius, the Old Latin Levit. 11. 13, 16 (Vulg. *accipiter*), and this; see also Rönsch, *It. V.* p. 521.
†*nigror* (concrete) 198. 1, 384. 19, equivalent to *puluis niger* 198. 8, 259. 19; cf. the classical *rubor* 198. 1, 8.
putramen, 247. 20 *putraminibus amputatis*, 684. 22 *neque enim sic putramina quaedam colliganda sunt ut* sq.[1]
seruitudo 328. 10. Only one doubtful passage of Livy is cited earlier.

---

[1] In 684. 22 the change from *colligenda* to *colliganda* is as easy as Hartel's (*Index*) suggestion of *putamina*, and gives better sense. It is the converse of *aperiendum uulnus est* in the other passage (247. 19), and an allusion to Cyprian's favourite metaphor of the falsely healed wound, though here the whole body of the Church, and not the individual Christian, is wounded. If *putamina* be read, how could the gathering up of branches already lopped inflict further damage upon the tree?

The Language of St. Cyprian. 303

Verbal nouns in -*tor* are :—

†*adulator* = 'deceiver' 745. 17. This, and not flatterer, must be the sense, and so probably also in 618. 1 *semper adulator ut fallat*; pleonasm is to be expected in Cyprian. Georges has this sense for *adulatio* from Quint. and Amm. Marc., but not for *adulator*. It occurs as the equivalent of ὑποκριτής in the fragmentary Latin translation of the Didache; see the Prolegomena to Harnack's edition, p. 278.

*delictor 720. 17, Paucker, *Suppl.* cites Commod. *Instr.* 53 (ii. 11. 5 Dombart), Hieron., Aug.

*inpugnator 615. 6, 689. 4. Cf. Paucker, *Nachträge*, p. 21.

*munerator 345. 1. Omitted by Georges; Salvian, Paul. Nol. (Paucker, *Subrelicta*).

occisor 734. 13. Plautus and Petilian (Georges).

palpator 13. 10. Plautus and Cassian, *Coll.* 10. 13 (Paucker, *Kl. Beitr.*).

Of the fourth and fifth declensions there are few words to be noticed. Cyprian has no such devotion to the fourth as has, for instance, Gellius.

†*congestus* 688. 2, see p. 271. Probably the dais on which were the altar and the seats for the clergy, but perhaps the assembly of clergy. No similar use seems to be cited.

†*ductus temporis longus* 576. 21. Nothing similar seems to be cited.

†*potentatus improbus* = 'exercise of power,' 'tyranny,' 588. 5. Another strange use is 340. 21.

primatus (pl.) = 'birthright' 411. 3, 798. 7. This must be the Old Latin reading of Gen. 25. 31, &c., cf. Tert. *De Ieiun.* 17, Ambr. *Ep.* 63. 99. The Vulgate has *primogenita*. It is not noticed by Rönsch or Georges.

§ 34. Adjectives, strange in form, or strangely used, are common :—

†*abhorrens* = 'repulsive' 569. 20; not in Georges, and no other example given in Wölfflin's *Archiv*, 4. 285.

†*alienus sensus* = 'insane' 681. 12. Georges only cites Firm. *Math.* 3. 6.

*balabundus 602. 20. There can be no doubt of the reading, though the word occurs nowhere else. Cornelius (611. 3) alludes to the passage, and corrects to *palabundus*, which Cyprian, with his love of synonyms, no doubt meant to write[1].

†*centenus fructus* = *centuplex* 832. 19. Georges only has Ven. Fort. 3. 9. 105 *centenus reditus*[2].

*cruciabundus 670. 7, apparently another ἅπαξ λεγόμενον.

†*discissa aemulatio* 604. 14 = *schismatica* : cf. *scissus error* 599. 1. Both must be attempts to provide a Latin equivalent for a Greek adjective.

*elucidus 598. 3. Not in Georges; but the reading is not quite certain.

†*expensa moderatio* 570. 20 ; cf. *pensius consilium* 649. 24.

*†*fluctuabundus* 255. 12. Ambr., Aug. (Georges)[3].

*indocibilis 253. 2, if this be the true reading. Wrongly cited by Ronsch *It. V.* from Iren. 4. 28; it is in neither Stieren's nor Harvey's index to Irenaeus.

*inlapsa firmitas 7. 3. Omitted by Georges.

†*inmerens* 256. 13 = 'guilty,' 'unworthy of reward'; not in Georges.

inpetrabilis et efficax sermo 271. 21. Plautus and Amm. Marc. Can this be an allusion to Jac. 5. 16 or Heb. 4. 12 ?

†*laudabilis* = ' laudatory '; 506. 8 *Nomen Dei laudabili testimonio praedicatur*, 598. 13 *delecti et ordinati et laudabili multorum sententia conprobati*, and similarly 629. 7, 20[4]. *Laudabile testimonium* is simply for *laus*. No one seems to have noticed this sense.

*mensurnus 571. 2, 585. 2. Novatian. *Trin.* 1, but apparently not earlier.

---

[1] Cf. Fronto, *Ad M. Caes.* 2. 12 (written by Marcus) *oues ... palantes balantesque oberrant*. *Palabundus* also is very rare. In *Quod Id.* 10 (27. 14) it is borrowed from Tert. *Apol.* 21.

[2] Cf. 202. 15 *fructus cum centeno*, from which agricultural formula *centenus fructus* is derived; Cic. *Verr.* 3. 47 *ager efficit cum octauo, bene ut agatur, nerum, ut omnes dii adiuuent, cum decumo* (cited from Roby, *Latin Gr.* § 1883). In 763 25 Cyprian uses *tricesimus, sexagesimus, centesimus* in the same sense, as in the Vulg. Mt. 13. 8 ; and in 202 15, 832 19 *sexagenarius fructus*.

[3] Beside the three *-bundus* forms given above, Cyprian has *gaudibundus* 831. 16 (Apul.) and *nutabundus* 5. 2 (literal in Apul , but not cited in Cyprian's metaphorical sense before Lact.) , also the common forms *cunctabundus* 829. 22, *errabundus* 773. 1, *furibundus* 617. 20, *gratulabundus* 621 9. The last is equivalent to *laetus*, as *gratulari* 691. 13 and often, *gratulatio* 615. 15 to *gaudere, gaudium*, for which cf. Ronsch, *It. V.* p 367, *Beitr.* 1. p 35

[4] Cf. Apul. *Flor.* 1. 9. 38 *utinam possem ... praedicabili testimonio tuo ad omnem nostram Camenam frui*, i. e. *laude*.

pertinax = *crudelis*, 637. 20. Georges only cites for this sense Capit. *Macr.* 13. 3, but it also occurs in Sen. *Ep.* 104. 29 *M. Catonem recentiorem cum quo et infestius fortuna egit et pertinacius.* Cf. *pertinacia* 600. 2.

*semitonsus 830. 6, and copied by Nemesianus 835. 15. For the subject cf. Friedländer's *D..rst.* 3. 518, who only refers to this and Artemidorus, *Oneirocr* 1. 21; Apul. *Met.* 9. 12 (162. 13 Eyss.) *capillum semirasi.*

separ 750. 4 *speciatim separes posuit.* Apparently the first example in prose; previously in the Silver poets only. Solinus and Priscian (Georges).

*septiformis 53. 17, 338. 3. Aug., Ambr., &c.

*serpentinus 431. 15, 806. 9; *De Aleatt.* 6 (A 98. 4). Aug., &c. Cf. Rönsch, *Collect.* 181, where is an instance, apparently literal, which may be earlier.

subtristis 498. 11. Ter., Amm. Marc., Hieron. (Georges).

†*uirginalis continentia* (of Cornelius, in the sense of Apoc. 14. 4) 629. 15. This seems the earliest example.

unanimis (never *unanimus*) 431. 5, 570. 6, 628. 21, 777. 13. In these Hartel gives no variant, but in 694. 16 and 754. 3 (the latter Biblical) the evidence is strong for *unianimis*, and the critical note to the latter passage leads to the suspicion that this may be the true reading elsewhere. For *unianimis* Georges has nothing earlier than the Scholia to Juvenal (5. 134), nor for *unanimis* than the Old Latin and Claudian; cf. Rönsch, *Collect.* p. 106. Cyprian has *semianimis* 595. 11 and 635. 19, and it is therefore more than probable that *exanime* should be read in 378. 1, not *exanimae*. Otherwise his constant adherence to -*animis* forms would be broken.

For adjectives used as substantives see p. 216. A few more may be given, and especially the names of the seasons, *hibernum, uernum, autumnum* 577. 14, 353. 1, 2[1], *magnalia* and *mirabilia* for miracles (see Hartel's *Index* and p. 245), *accidentia* 363. 21, cited only from Quint. *Decl.* and Amm.

[1] All these occur in Tertullian; see Oehler's *Index*. Amid all that has been written about them the Carthaginian mosaic *C. I. L.* 8. 12558, giving the names *autumnus, aestas, iemns, uernus*, does not seem to have been noticed. Nowhere else does *uernus* masc. occur. For the neuter cf. *diurna* (pl.) = *dies*, Cael. Aur. *Acut.* 2. 39. 228 (Georges). I have already suggested that 577. 14 may be a reminiscence of Virg. *Aen.* 1. 266.

Marc., *populares* = 'commons' 673. 16, which the dictionaries only cite from *Hist. Aug.*, Amm. Marc., and later Jct., though it already occurs in Tert. *Spect.* 3, *masculus*, always a substantive in Cyprian, 190. 13, 16, 203. 6, 468. 10, 473. 3, 22, 476. 2 [1]. For the elliptical *dominicus* (*dies*), and *dominicum* and *sanctum* (*sacrificium*), see pp. 245, 266. A curious ellipse is 36. 20 *de diuinis fontibus inpleuimus modicum*.

§ 35. Of the pronouns little can be said without touching upon syntax. Generally speaking it may be said that his use of them is that of his age. *Hic* for *is*, *iste* (in Roman as well as in African writing) for *hic*, *ipse* for *idem* (cf. Sittl, *Lok. Verschiedenheiten* 115, Rönsch, *Beitr.* 2. 26), *alius* for *alter*, *quis* for *uter* were to be expected [2]. The rarity of -*met* forms (e.g. 226. 1 and 477. 16, where *semet* should surely be read instead of *se et*) is noticeable; *sese* is never used. Indefinite *quis* is widely and often strangely used; *Test.* 3. 25 *tit.*, 8. 5, 263. 3, 807. 12, &c. *Quidam* (cf. Petschenig in Wölfflin's *Archiv*, 6. 268 for the use in Amm. Marc.) is constantly used for *sunt qui*, *nonnulli*; 297. 7, 616. 18, 722. 1, &c. *Quisque* and *quicumque* are often used for *quiuis* (see Hartel's *Index*, and for *quicumque* add 799. 15 (Stephanus) and 809. 16), but the chief use of *quisque* is of course for *quicumque*, which, in the classical use, is rare. *Quidquid*, however, is always used, and never *quidque* in this sense. *Quisquis* is rare (add 12. 11, *Sent.* 18). *Quispiam*, *quiuis*, *quilibet* are, I think, never used. *Singuli*, with and without *quique*, is a favourite substitute for *omnes*; *unusquisque* also is common. *Eiusmodi* stands alone for *talis*, and more rarely as an attribute; 219. 5, 225. 15, 241. 4, 468. 4, 694. 15, &c., but is not frequent. *Huiusmodi* is very rare, perhaps only in 226. 1. Kalb, *Roms Juristen*, p. 108, notes that *huiusmodi* does not prevail till after Papinian in legal Latin.

To express reciprocation Cyprian uses *inuicem*, I think, nineteen times; with an accusative *Test.* 3. 9 *tit.*, 408. 13,

---

[1] *Mares* only 10. 10 It had probably died out of the spoken language.

[2] Hartel's *Index* is by no means complete in these respects.

The Language of St. Cyprian. 307

427. 17, 643. 6, 668. 8; a genitive 695. 3; dative 217. 22, 240. 24, 243. 8 (706. 2 shows that this is dative), 501. 9, 689. 12, 712. 1, 733. 10; ablative (*separare, recedere ab inuicem*) 364. 18, 475. 23, 476. 9, 711. 18. The only other prepositions so used are *aduersum* 278. 13, and *cum* 650. 16. *Utrubique* (for which Haussleiter in Wölfflin's *Archiv*, 5. 565 suggests *utrumque*), 695. 4, *mutuo* 677. 2 (cf. 689. 12), and *in unum* 678. 9 are isolated instances; *alterutrum* 799. 17 is a citation from Stephanus. Reflexive pronouns alone are used for reciprocation 240. 24, 712. 4, and similarly a personal pronoun 508. 17. Beside these may be mentioned 645. 21 *alius pro altero*, 699. 17 *unusquisque pro altero*[1].

§ 36. Cyprian is more bold in the use of verbs than in that of nouns, and the number of new and rare forms is somewhat large. But it is in their syntax, with which this paper is not concerned, that he is most original and inventive.

abalienari = 'wander in mind' 289. 23. Haussleiter in Wölfflin's *Archiv*, 1. 870 cites only this and two isolated Biblical readings, Jerem. 23. 7 (Wirceb.) and Mc. 4. 19 (Colbert.).

*abigeare 773. 1. Though *abigeator* and *abigeatus* (n.) occur, this verb does not seem to recur even in glosses.

*amoenare 4. 1. Cassiod., Salvian, &c.

circumcursare 683. 22. Plaut., Ter., Lucr., Lact., &c.

†*clarificare* 679. 4 *clarificato die*. There seems to be nothing like this.

†*coagulare* (metaphorical) 226. 18 *coagulati cum isdem simul ad audaciam*.

contestari = *declarare*; in citations of Scripture as 192. 22 *contestans ait*, 758. 14, &c.; with acc. inf. often 309. 18, 360. 26, 588. 11 (double acc.), 740. 23, &c., and with *quod* 634. 8; with acc. 270. 1 *contestari peccata*, 692. 10 *merita*, 222. 13, &c.; with acc. also in the Roman *Epp.* 551. 2, 559. 15. It

---

[1] No grammatical paper could be more admirable than Thielmann's on this subject in the *Archiv*, 7. 343 ff. He says that *inuicem* occurs about twenty times in Cyprian, the classical *inter se* once. This is an oversight, for it actually occurs in the Roman *Ep.* 36 (575. 6), if it be the true reading. Other noteworthy instances of reciprocation not written by Cyprian are 335. 16, 530. 11, 554. 5, 575. 8, 637. 1, 810. 6, 811. 1. 814. 7, 836. 1.

is Biblical with acc. inf. (e. g. 1 Pet. 5. 12), but does not occur in the Vulgate with an acc. of the thing attested, nor in Cyprian with a personal object (*contestor uos*) as is usual in the Vulgate. Jerome seems the first writer after Cyprian freely to use the word as he does. Aug. and Ambr. appear to avoid it. In the strange *contestantes ei* 731. 18 both case and pronoun seem to be chosen simply for rhyme.

dilucidare: 589. 2 *dilucidata ueritate*. This must be the reading, as in Tert. *Marc*. 3. 23 *init*.; cf. Paucker's *Ergänzungen I*.

euirare (literal) 10. 10. Varro, Catullus, Arnob. 5. 42 (211. 23 Reiff.).

gratulari=laetari; add 8. 16, 545. 6, 588. 12, 641. 10, 740. 17, cf. Rönsch, *It. V.* p. 367, and Dante, *Parad*. 24. 149. Gratulatio 615. 15. *gratulabundus* 621. 9, in the same sense; cf. *gratulanter* in Paucker, *Addenda*.

†*laxare* (*pacem*, &c. *alicui*), add 625. 16, 637. 21, 638. 8, 16. I can find no parallel.

leuare; 630. 18 *cum multo patientius et tolerabilius audiret* (Decius) *leuari aduersum se aemulum principem quam constitui Romae Dei sacerdotem*. The only resemblance seems to be 2 Esdr. 6. 6 *et leuare te uelis super eos regem*.

†*limare*, see Hartel's *Index*. The meaning seems to be to form a decision, not to enquire into a proposal; e. g 596. 25, where otherwise would be an awkward ὕστερον πρότερον.

lucrari=effugere (*manus carnificis*, &c.) 306. 23, 342. 3, 619. 12; cf. *lucrum* 312. 27. Apul. *Met*. 8. 12 (142. 12 Eyss), Amm. Marc. 19. 4. 3, Victor Vit. 3. 26 (84. 22 Petsch.); so *lucri facere* in *Bell. Hisp*. 36. 1, Tert. *Res. Carn*. 42, &c., and *lucratio* Tert. *Test. An*. 4 (139. 17 Reiff.).

†*portare*; (1) *Christum hominem portabat* of the Incarnation; see p. 248. This phrase is Cyprian's own; it is not in Tertullian or Irenaeus, and does not seem to be adopted by later writers[1]. (2) *Portare typum, figuram*, &c., see p. 254;

---

[1] Cf. *baiulare* in Iren. 5. 19. 1 *sua propria eum (Dominum) baiulante conditione, quae baiulatur ab ipso*, though the sense is different. Father Puller, S. S. J. E., has pointed out to me the use of *portare* in Iren. 5. 18. 1 *Pater conditionem simul et Verbum suum portans*, and that it is only another step (though Irenaeus does not seem to take it) to speak of the Church being borne by the Word. Irenaeus prefers *recapitulare* in this connexion, as in 5. 20. 2. Tertullian has *specie hominis quam erat gestaturus* in *Adu. Marc*. 4. 22, and *gestare* also *ib*. 34 and *Carn. Xti* 10, &c. *Gestabat* for *portabat* is the

The Language of St. Cyprian. 309

this again seems peculiar to Cyprian. (3) *Portare peccata*, in the usual Christian sense.

†*praeformare = praefigurare* 217. 4. Nothing like it is cited.

propagare = crescere 7. 19 *immundos spiritus . . . incremento poenae propagantis extendere*, copied in *Quod Id.* (25. 7). It seems to be intransitive, and synonymous with *incremento*; so Léonard, who gives no parallel[1].

*quaestionare 732. 2. Absent in the Vatican Fragments of Jurisprudence, from which Georges cites it.

recalcitrare = rebellare 423. 14. Bibl. (only Deut. 32. 15), Amm. Marc.

†*recreare* (of Baptism), see p. 264. Cyprian is the first to use it in this sense.

†*reparare* (*aliquem*) 273. 6, 362. 27, 373. 5, 394. 9, 400. 27 and (in *Ep.* 75) 821. 31. Cf. Min. Fel. 34. 12 (49. 24 Halm). Cyprian is the first to use this verb also of Baptism, and almost the first to use it with a personal object.

†*repraesentare = reddere* 542. 15, 596. 21, 808. 12; cf. Hartel's *Index* to Lucifer. Another strange use is 502. 13 *officium meum uestra diligentia repraesentet*, for which Greg. M. *Ep.* I. 1 *nostra per eum repraesentetur auctoritas* (Lewis and Short) is the only parallel cited; yet cf. O. Ritschl, *Cyprian v. Carthago*, p. 11 ff. In ordinary senses the verb is very common, as it is in Seneca. Perhaps this is one of Cyprian's debts to him.

†*reseruare = saluare*, see p. 249. Also *= obseruare* (*legem*, &c.) 284. 2, 513. 10, 713. 19.

†*satiare = abundanter addere* (Hartel) 755, 15. This and the similar passages from the *Vita* 8 and *Sing. Cler.* 8 seem to stand alone, while the sense of *adiuuare*, 377. 16, is quite isolated.

siccare intrans. 808. 8. Lact. 7. 3. 8, where Bünemann's instances from Apicius are copied by Georges.

†*solidare* (*fidem*, &c.) 494. 6, 579. 8. In other remarkable senses 304. 23, 318. 11, 675. 1, 712. 6, and in *Ep.* 75 (820. 27). Cyprian is not only the first but the boldest employer of this word in metaphorical senses. Lact., *Epit.* 66. 8, *Opif.*

---

reading of the Oxford MS. Bodl. Add. C. 15, of the beginning of the tenth century, in 711. 12. *Induere* in this sense is confined to *Quod Id.*, 28. 9, 31. 3.

[1] But could it be synonymous with *extendere*, describing further the use of the *eculeus*?

310 The Style and Language of St. Cyprian.

10. 9, imitates him. The passage in *Ep.* 75 is one of many signs that Cyprian had a hand in that letter.

*sordidare ; add 201. 5, 219. 21, 374. 24, 830. 3 (literal), and *Sent.* 42. Lact., Hieron. (*Ep.* 54. 16 as well as 107. 10, which is cited by Georges), Firm. *Math.*, &c.

†*sospitare* = *saluare* 188. 25, 211. 9. Enn., Pacuv., Plaut., Catull., Liv., &c., but very rare. This attempt of Cyprian's to enrich theological diction was unsuccessful ; see p. 249.

*sportulare 466. 12 ; ἅπ. λεγ. ; see p. 274. It must mean to give, and not to receive, the *sportula*, as the dictionaries would have it.

subitare = 'take by surprise' 693. 15. The only other instances seem to be the *Vita*, § 15 (cvi. 17), and Apoc. 3. 3 (Primasius) *ueniam et subitabo aduentum meum.* Cf. *subitatio* in Sap. 5. 2, and *desubitare* Firm. *Math.* 3. 4. 6 (cited in Paucker, *Addenda*). See Wölfflin's *Archiv*, 3. 255 and 4. 586.

taxare = *indicare* 705. 19. So Tert. *Praescr.* 6, *Adu. Marc.* 4. 20, 27, though usually in Tert. it means to blame. This is its only occurrence in Cyprian, and is a sign that when *Ep.* 63 was written he was still under Tertullian's influence; cf. p. 199.

*turificare : only the perf. part. *turificati* is used 624. 19. Cf. Paucker's *Ergänzungen II.*

†*uentilare honorem* 340. 9 ; cf. Juv. 1. 28 ; in the opposite sense 598. 14 ; *uentilare mendacia* 678. 12, as in Min. Fel. 28. 2, Tert., &c. ; to spread a rumour 628. 18, 839. 14 ; add to Hartel's list 211. 3 (literal).

Beside these there are two possible readings which should be mentioned :—

dereputare 253. 12 *delicta nostra dereputemus* (S¹). The alliteration makes it the more probable.

exabundare, almost certainly in 353. 15, 411. 23 ; see Hartel's critical notes, and Quicherat's *Addenda*.

It is probable also that in 727. 21 there is a verb *gloriare* = *glorificare*, see p. 223.

---

augere intrans. 643. 2. Rönsch, *Beitr.* 3. 9 only cites Jerem. 22. 30 in Iren. 3. 29 and a gloss.

*coniacere 475. 5. Cf. Paucker, *Ergänzungen I*¹.

[1] The other verbs of this form in Cyprian are *condolere* 521. 11, *congaudere*

manere = κοιμᾶσθαι 473. 3, 475. 21 ; = *habitare* 370. 8, 410. 22 (the latter pleonastic *habitare et manere*) ; see Ronsch, *Beitr.* 3. 57 f. for both senses.

---

animadvertere aliquem; add 839. 16 to Hartel's list, perhaps the earliest instances with a direct personal object; Fronto, p. 207 Naber, cited by Hartel, *peruerse facta animaduertit* is not to the point.

†*concludere* = 'choke' 256. 2, 357. 18 ; cf. 373. 17. Cited by Georges only from Palladius.

†*conlidere* intrans. 215. 8, and in the Roman *Ep.* 36 (573. 21). S. Brandt in Wölfflin's *Archiv*, 8, p. 130 cites Lact. *Inst.* 2. 8. 31, *De Ira* 10. 25.

consistere (see Hartel's *Index*) in the present part. is constantly used in the Christian sense of sojourning, as in the newly-discovered translation of Clement, § 1, παροικῶν. This is not a Biblical usage[1]. Unless (as Harnack asserts) Clement was a translation of the second century, these instances in Cyprian may be the earliest. *Consistens* is also twice used for Cyprian's favourite *constitutus*; in *Ep.* 17 *tit* (521. 2) *fratribus in plebe consistentibus*, and 749. 13 *extra ecclesiam consistens*[2].

†*depromere* = 'publish,' 'proclaim' 239. 21, 309. 26, 400. 13, 427. 20, 727. 13. Nothing like this seems to be cited except Nazarius, *Pan.* 8.

dirigere litteras ad aliquem 514. 5, 516. 13, 519. 14, 600. 12, 606. 9, 715. 9, 731. 17. Cf. Wölfflin in his *Archiv*, 4. 100, who knows no example between the Muratorian canon (p. 10 b., *9 epistulae autem Pauli quae a quo loco uel qua ex causa directae sint* sq.) and Jerome.

†*distribuere*; 277. 4 *exemplum discipulis suis distribuens* = *dans*; probably only chosen for the alliteration with *dis-*, without

---

620. 9, *conluctari* 431. 23, *conmori* 341. 15, *conpati* 521. 10, *consepultus* 740. 21, and the Biblical *consurgere* 429. 5 (see 428. 22). All of these are used earlier than Cyprian ; cf. Ronsch, *Collect.* 245.

[1] The use in the *Acta* of Cyprian by the proconsul Paternus (cx. 28) is the usual one ; cf. Mayor's Appendix to his Juvenal, p 390, on 3. 296.

[2] *Constitutus in, inter*, &c. = καθεστώς, &c., has been so fully and so well discussed by Kalb and others that there is no need to dwell upon it here. It is, of course, by no means peculiar to Cyprian. I may refer to a note which I have contributed to the edition of the Vulgate by Wordsworth and White on Joh. 5. 13.

thought of the appropriateness of the word; cf. 394. 6 con-
tribuens pro terrenis caelestia, which also simply means giving.

†incurrere supplicia, incommoda 342. 4, 364. 24. Lact., Arnob.,
&c.: see Bünemann on Lact. 2. 7. 23.

†obtendere 254. 8 quid caeci oculi paenitentiae iter non uident quod
obtendimus? This must be in the sense of ostendere, for which
perhaps it is only an error. Nothing like it seems to occur
elsewhere.

†offerre: oblati praefectis 840. 12, and Acta § 3 (cxii. 12).

praeligere 577. 1. This very rare word is only cited from Apul.
Met. 7. 11 (123. 25 Eyss.), and Tert. Ad Nat. 1. 14 (a false
reference in Oehler). But can it be discriminated from prae-
eligere? Cf. Rönsch, It. V. 210, Paucker, Ergänzungen II,
and Engelbrecht in Sitzungsber. of the Vienna Academy, vol.
110, on Claud. Mamertus.

†proponere = edicere 284. 15, and cf. 682. 16; proponere edictum
Novatian in Ep. 30 (551. 10), Tert. Pud. 1.

statuere = sistere 249. 13, 355. 25, 424. 3. Arnob. 1. 50 (34. 16
Reiff.), where Hildebrand only cites Cyprian; but cf. Rönsch,
Beitr. 3. 77 for Plautus and Propertius.

struere = instruere 598. 5; cf. Rönsch, It. V. 380, and Beitr. 3.
78, where he cites from Haupt an inscription given in Spicil.
Solesm. which copies 249. 13 (v. s) with struatur for statuatur[1].
If this reading be accepted, Cyprian's will be the earliest
instance in the sense of obstruere.

†transpungere: transpunctae mentis alienatione dementes 261. 17.
In this metaphorical sense of stricken, synonymous with
alienatio and demens, Cyprian seems to be the first to use the
verb, which is cited also from Cael. Aur., though transpunctio
261. 12, is biblical.

---

*exambire 528. 2, 630. 11, 739. 22, with different constructions.
Arnob. 3. 24, 7. 15, onwards.

ignire (literal) 339. 1. This was probably in Cyprian's Bible in
2 Macc. 7. 3 (Vulg. succendi); aurum ignitum 384. 10 is
Biblical; see ib. 6 and Rönsch, It. V. p. 156.

---

[1] This reading, and in 238. 8 quam uos laetos excipit from the same source
(Haupt, Opusc. 3. p. 202) are very tempting; but de oc mundo for de proelio
show that the latter at any rate is only a paraphrase. The change, of course,
was necessary in the case of a natural death, but when one change was made
another might easily be admitted.

The Language of St. Cyprian. 313

The only impersonal verb which appears first in Cyprian is:—

*horret 781. 18 *nec delectat id dicere quod aut horret aut pudet nosse.* This does not seem to be cited elsewhere; was it improvised by Cyprian for uniformity with *pudet* [1]?

Present participles used as substantives are not common: *aemulantes* = *aduersarii* 598. 14, *audientes* (see p. 263), *blandiens* = quack 570. 1, *commeantes* 746. 14, *confitentes* 615. 5, *credentes* (see p. 255), *delinquentes* 743. 4, *uenientes* = προσ-ήλυτοι (see p. 263). *Discens* for *discipulus* seems to be absent.

§ 37. Adverbs are used in extraordinary abundance, but not many seem to be new:—

*deuote = 'loyally' 513. 9. Lact., &c.
†plane = *certe, nimirum, utique,* but never, I think, for *perspicue, aperte,* as Hartel would have it in some instances. Add to his instances 338. 15, 748. 22, 776. 14 [2].

Cyprian, like Apuleius, delights in adverbs in -*im* :— [3]

glomeratim 479. 10. *Aetna* 199, Macr. *Sat.* 6. 4. 3 (where Jan has no note) onwards.
speciatim 750. 4 ; seven times in the *Hist. Aug.,* see Rönsch, *It. V.* p. 149, and Paucker, *Nachtrage,* p. 24.

---

[1] *Oportet* in Cyprian is always, except perhaps in 385. 12, used in the stronger sense of *necesse est*; the usual meaning being supplied by *conuenit,* &c.

[2] Cyprian also uses the rare forms *consulte* 475. 20, *exerte* 420. 11 (meaning clearly, not energetically ; a sense omitted by Georges, though used also by Tertullian), *inlicite* 643. 2, 757. 6, *secrete* 268. 23. He has no new forms in -*o* ; for *festinato, iterato, uero* = *uere,* see Hartel's *Index.*

[3] *Statim* in 229. 26, 250. 21, and 811. 6 (*Ep.* 75) is used in the sense of 'necessarily,' as in Sen. *Ep.* 45. 10. *Interim* must mean ' at once' in 475. 24, 636. 7, 647. 14 ; it usually has the sense of 'for the present,' or ' for a time,' as 244. 13, 659. 18. The other adverbs of this form used by Cyprian are *confestim* 542. 15, *gregatim* 541. 3, *nominatim* 516. 3, 12, *oppidatim* and *ostiatim* 598. 21, 22, *passim* often (in the sense of 'indiscriminately,' 269. 4), *priuatim* 271. 5, 512. 19, and in *Ep.* 75 (816. 21), *singillatim* 271. 4. Beside these *saltim* or *saltem* is used with *nec* or *non* instead of *ne* . . . *quidem* (cf. Sittl in *Jahresber.* 1892, p. 235) in 241. 14, 242. 11, 360. 9, 402. 25, 826. 8 ; without a negative, only 14. 12 and 604. 15.

314   *The Style and Language of St. Cyprian.*

The following in *-ter* are noteworthy :—

granditer five times ; see Hartel's *Index*. Only two eailier instances of this adverb are cited from Ovid, and 1 Esdr. 9. 7 from *Cod. Tolet.* (Rönsch, *It. V.* p. 150.)
*inseparabiliter 215. 11, 22, 278. 2.   Lact., Hieron., Aug.
*saeculariter Test. 3. 36 *tit.*   Aug., Prosper.
†*subtiliter fallens* 289. 20 ; cf. *subtilitas* in Rönsch, *Beitr.* 1. 68; in the usual sense 782. 21.

Derived from present participles are :—
†*exultanter* 614. 11, 691. 9.
*gubernanter 608. 10.   Omitted by Georges.
ignoranter 701. 16, 715. 3 ; only Vulg. (Old Latin) Ecclus. 14. 7 ; Rufinus, Aug.
indesinenter 733. 20. Vulg. only Heb. 10. 1. Lucifer, Hieron., &c.
*urgenter 676. 14 and in the Roman *Ep.* 36 (573. 4).   Aug.

Of temporal adverbs and conjunctions the rarity of *saepe* has already been noticed on p. 220. The same has been noted by Wölfflin in Cassius Felix ; but Cyprian never uses the comparative or superlative of *frequenter* ; *saepius* and *saepissime* are always used. *Iugiter*, also as in Cassius Felix, alternates with *semper*. *Mox* is never used ; its place is taken by *cito* or *uelociter*[1]. The strange use of *retro* for 'in future' occurs in 366. 13.   *Tunc* is always used, and never *tum*.

There is less to be said about local words. *Exinde*, rare in this sense, occurs 841. 13, 15 ; *istic, istinc* always mean 'here' and 'hence,' and with *illic, illinc* are constantly used of Carthage and Rome[2]. *Istic* for *istuc* 616. 11, but *illuc* 725. 15. *Nusquam* is put strangely for *nequaquam* in 394. 26, and the curious form of question *ubi erit quod . . . ?* occurs several times, as 601. 10 *ubi erit quod discimus ?*, 634. 20, 793. 12, 15 ; so in *Ep.* 75 (824. 17) and in Roman *Epp.* 551. 22, 562. 15, 564. 6.

[1] *Mox* in the Vulgate is confined to six examples, five of which are in books not revised by Jerome.

[2] For the pleonastic *illinc ab urbe*, &c., see p. 238   Here may be mentioned the attributive use of *illic, istic,* and *quondam,* indexed by Hartel ; add to these *postmodum* 375. 14, *semper* 241. 23, and perhaps *statim* 505. 14.   In *Ep.* 75 occur *retro* 816. 25, and *foris* 822. 11.

The Language of St. Cyprian. 315

Fortasse (239. 6, 307. 18), *fortassis* (475. 8 and in the Roman *Ep.* 31, 558. 7) and *forsitan* (254. 2 and fairly often), are all used, as in Apuleius; cf. Becker, *Stud. Apul.* p. 11.

Among negatives *haud* is absent, though common in the artificial style of Arnobius. *Neue* is also absent, being replaced by *neque, et* or *aut*; once *ne . . . uel ne* 500. 14, and twice probably *ne . . . ne* in co-ordinate clauses, 588. 3[1], 688. 16. *Non* forming one notion with the word connected, adjective, adverb, &c. is characteristic of Cyprian; *non salubriter* 195. 16, *non de eius sententia ordinati = contra* 672. 16, *de non colentibus* 361. 11, &c. *Necdum* and *neque enim* have quite taken the place of *nondum, non enim*; hence *et necdum, necdum quoque* 593. 8, 801. 4, *neque enim et* 688. 10. But irregular negatives are countless.

Of irregularly used copulative conjunctions some examples have been given on pp. 230, 239. It may be stated as a general rule that *et* connects clauses, *ac* words. *Item* is excessively common. *Aut . . . aut* is used for *et . . . et* or *tam . . . quam* in 240. 14, 548. 5, 673. 20, and often, though *uel . . . uel* is normal in this sense, 356. 19, &c. The comparative particles are *tantum . . . quantum* or *in tantum . . . in quantum*; *tam . . . quam, hoc . . . quo* and *tanto . . . quanto* are rarer[2]. But the most noteworthy and almost the most common of Cyprian's usages are those of *et* for *sed* or *tamen* either at the beginning or in the middle of a sentence. Only once is it used between words, not clauses, 283. 2, unless *et* be read in 586. 2; but such expressions as 263. 11 *distribuendum per apostolos totum* (all they had) *dabant et non talia delicta redimebant* and 366. 12 are of constant occurrence. Conversely *sed et* in similar positions, well, though not completely, indexed by Hartel, is frequently used for *et*.

---

[1] Hartel once, 588. 3, reads *neue*, but the text is doubtful, and it seems better to read *ne . . . ne* as suggested above.

[2] *Quam amplior . . . tam maior* 14. 21. *Quantum . . . tantum* with positive adj. 262. 16, 584. 10. Other instances are 490. 8, 505. 2, 546. 22. For *in tantum . . . in quantum* and variants see Hartel *s. vv. in* and *quantus*. *Quanto* with *tanto* omitted 189. 17.

Of adversative conjunctions, *immo*, in various positions, is very common [1]. *Porro* also is frequent, always initial and usually with *autem* [2]. *At* (*at enim* 301. 7, *at uero* 651. 24) appears to be almost extinct. For *sed enim* see Hartel's *Index*. *Ceterum* is very common at the beginning of periods in a strongly adversative sense. *Certe* is always initial (227. 16, 601. 8, &c.), and used not for restriction, but for assertion. *Ergo* is apparently used for *tamen* in a conversational passage, 307. 18, as it is in *Sent.* 4 (438. 3).

Nisi si is constantly used with the indicative in a *reductio ad absurdum*, as 382. 20; only 334. 8, 496. 15 in another sense with the subjunctive. *Si* is strangely used for *quod* in 249. 23, 468. 7, 740. 17. *Dum* is often used, and invariably with the present indicative, as a causal particle; *dummodo* perhaps only 779. 12 [3].

In the place of the old conclusive particles, *hinc, inde, unde* are almost always used. *Propter quod* and *et idcirco* are much more common than *quamobrem, quare* or *quapropter*, though all these occur; *quocirca* is absent. *Denique* in several senses —for instance, 'in consequence,' 'accordingly,' and as a simple copula—rarely in that of 'finally,' is very common [4], e.g. 421. 23, 501. 1, 618. 4, 700. 11.

Probably no writer has used *quominus* so freely as Cyprian in all connexions; e.g. 260. 3, 297. 11, 411. 9, 502. 18. Final *ut*, as has been said, is rare unless strengthened with *ad hoc, propter hoc*, &c. But the use of *ut* as simply explanatory or consecutive is a marked feature in his style; 195. 23, 312. 21, 26, 522. 15, 794. 18, &c.

Clauses with *quia, quod, quoniam* for the acc. inf. are, of

---

[1] It is used for *potius*; *nemo cogitet . . . sed immo consideret* 334. 3, and 219. 22.

[2] *Porro autem* = 'on the contrary' 797. 8; cf. Ronsch, *Beitr.* 2. 78.

[3] The combinations of *dum*, &c. are often curious; *dum . . . sic* 743. 16, 772. 5, *sic . . . dum* 605. 1, *hinc . . . dum* 423. 9, *inde . . . dum* 422. 17, *co . . . dum* 212. 3, *inde . . . quod* or *quia* 362. 30, 408. 9, 667. 20, 798. 7.

[4] Cf. Kalb, *Roms Juristen*, p. 19 f., Becker, *Stud Apul.* p. 32, Ronsch, *Beitr.* 2. 65.

The Language of St. Cyprian. 317

course, common in a writer of the third century, and most of them have been indexed by Hartel.

§ 38. The most remarkable part of Cyprian's syntax is that of prepositions, which must be omitted here. He avoids both archaic and vulgar forms; several which are common in such writers as Fronto and Tertullian, and used by other writers in Cyprian's correspondence, are absent. The following are not used:—*absque* (but *abs* 253. 24, 676. 11), *cis*, *citra*, *clam* (though *coram* is used as a preposition, and *palam* as an adverb), *erga* and *ergo*, *penes*, *pone*, *prae*, *secus*, *subter*, *tenus*, *usque* and *adusque*[1]. *Trans* is confined to the formula *trans mare constituti* 592. 22, 601. 3; *ex* and *ob* are comparatively rare, while *apud* has an extraordinary extension of meaning.

The following ablatives are used with the genitive as substitutes for prepositions:—*beneficio* 385. 21[2], *causa* 659. 27, *fraude* 769. 12, *merito* (cf. Sittl, *op. cit.* p. 135), 711. 4, *respectu* 510. 5. To these should perhaps be added *fide* 281, 4, 303. 3, 357. 16, 370. 12, and *ui* 302. 16, 305. 16.

There is little to be said about exclamations. *Utinam* 517. 15, &c. is varied thrice by the poetical *o si* 10. 24, 361. 18. 685. 6; except in 253. 23, where there is the accusative, *o* is followed by the nominative 14. 1, 9, &c. *Pro dolor* occurs 9. 12, 243. 19, *pro nefas* 199. 10, 242. 10. *Oro, quaeso, puta*, are used without construction, as in other writers.

---

[1] *Usque ad* 256. 16, 401. 26, 402. 6, 503. 10, 764. 3; *ad finem usque* 503. 7.

[2] Cyprian may have learnt this use from Seneca, who has it frequently. *Dial.* 5. 2. 1 &c. It is also used by Apuleius, *Met* 5. 25, 8. 20 (93. 15, 147, 6 Eyss.) and Ps.-Apul *Ascl.* 31 (54. 12 Goldbacher), and by Lucianus 533 7. Sittl, *Lok. Verschied*, p. 136, strangely seems to regard it as African, and the instance in the *Tita* (A. c. 10) as the earliest. At any rate he quotes no other. See also Wolfflin's *Archiv*, 8. 590.

TEXTUAL SUGGESTIONS.

Hartel 338. 17	. . Page	256
370. 17	. . . .	212
378. 1	. . . .	305
402. 21	. . . .	266 n.
477. 16	. . . .	306
483. 10	. . . .	220 n.
501. 17	. . . .	234 n.
524. 5	. . . .	282 n.
531. 12	. . . .	260 n.
552. 8	. . . .	210 n.
582. 22	. . . .	213 n.
588. 3	. . . .	315 n.

Hartel 589. 2	. . Page	308
623. 6	. . .	235
633. 14	. . . .	220 n.
646. 20	. . . .	213 n.
684. 22	. . . .	302 n.
711. 22	. . . .	220 n.
736. 11	. . . .	247
746. 11	. . . .	213 n.
779. 2	. . . .	220 n.
794. 4	. . . .	221 n.
835. 3	. . . .	210 n.

www.ingramcontent.com/pod-product-compliance
Lightning Source LLC
Chambersburg PA
CBHW021833300426
44114CB00009BA/426